365

activities
you and your child
will love

GYMBOREE PLAY & MUSIC

365

activities

you and your child will love

author
nancy wilson hall

consulting editors
dr. roni cohen leiderman & dr. wendy masi

illustrator
christine coirault

photographer
john robbins

KEY PORTER BOOKS

Produced by Weldon Owen Inc.,
814 Montgomery Street, San Francisco, California 94133,
in collaboration with the Gymboree Corporation, Inc.,
500 Howard Street, San Francisco, California 94105.

Gymboree Play & Music

Chief Executive Officer **Matthew McCauley**
Vice President, Gymboree Play & Music **Jill Johnston**
Merchandise Manager **Dawn Sagorski**
Senior Program Developer **Helene Silver Freda**

Weldon Owen Group

Chief Executive Officer **John Owen**

Weldon Owen Inc.

Chief Executive Officer, President **Terry Newell**
Vice President, Publisher **Roger Shaw**
Vice President, Creative Director **Gaye Allen**
Vice President, International Sales **Stuart Laurence**
Production Director **Chris Hemesath**

Executive Editor **Elizabeth Dougherty**
Editor **Karen Penzes**
Contributing Editor **Maria Behan**
Assistant Editor **Lucie Parker**
Editorial Assistant **Mary Colgan**
Copy Editor **Jacqueline K. Aaron**
Proofreaders **Gail Nelson-Bonebrake, Marisa Solís**
Indexer **Ken DellaPenta**

Art Director **Lisa Milestone**
Designers **Britt Staebler, Renée Myers**
Photo Manager **Meghan Hildebrand**
Photographer's Assistant **Dan Jenkins**

Key Porter Books Limited

Six Adelaide Street East, Tenth Floor
Toronto, Ontario Canada M5C 1H6

Library and Archives Canada Cataloguing in Publication

Hall, Nancy
365 activities for you and your child/
Nancy Hall. 1. Preschool children—
Recreation. 2. Games. 3. Creative activities
and seat work. 4. Amusements. I. Title. II.
Title: Three hundred sixty-five activities for
you and your child.

GV1201.H323 2007   649'.5
C2007-900880-1

THE CANADA COUNCIL | LE CONSEIL DES ARTS   ONTARIO ARTS COUNCIL
FOR THE ARTS | DU CANADA   CONSEIL DES ARTS DE L'ONTARIO
SINCE 1957 | DEPUIS 1957

ISBN-13 978-1-55263-881-1
ISBN-10 1-55263-881-2

Printed in China.

a special note on safety

At Gymboree, we encourage parents to become active play partners with their children. As you enjoy these enriching activities with your child, please make safety your priority. While the risk of injury during any of these activities is low, please take every precaution to ensure that your child is safe at all times.

To reduce the risk of injury, please follow these guidelines: do not leave your child unattended, even for a brief moment, during any of the activities in this book; be particularly cautious when participating in the activities involving water because of the risk of drowning; ensure that your child does not place in his or her mouth any small objects (even those depicted in the photographs and illustrations), as some may pose a choking hazard and could be fatal if ingested; and make sure that writing and craft materials are nontoxic and have been approved for use by children.

Throughout this book, we have suggested guidelines on the age appropriateness of each activity; however, it is up to you to assess the suitability of a particular activity for your child before attempting it. Ability, balance, and dexterity vary considerably from child to child, even among children of the same age.

While we have made every effort to ensure that the information is accurate and reliable, and that the activities are safe and workable when an adult is properly supervising, we disclaim all liability for any unintended, unforeseen, or improper application of the recommendations and suggestions featured in this book.

contents

five
years & up

244

Foreword

Welcome to the world of preschoolers! From ages three through five, language skills explode, imagination soars, and independence grows. This is a time of wonder, fun, and adventures big and small.

Your child will begin to have long conversations and tell elaborate stories, sing just to express joy, gain strength and a sense of physical mastery, develop an amazing sense of humor, and still cuddle you close at the end of his or her delightfully busy day.

Preschoolers have an increased enthusiasm for new experiences. Improved memory, coordination, and problem-solving skills extend their repertoire of play. Whether your child's favorite activities involve games, art, music, or physical challenges, learning through play is the best—and the most fun—way to boost brainpower and expand interests.

This book gives you a road map of wonderful activities to share with your child, but your creative preschooler will take you on many off-road adventures, bringing our suggestions to life in ways that we haven't even begun to imagine. Enjoy the journey—and take the time to treasure these magical years.

Dr. Roni Cohen Leiderman
Dr. Wendy Masi

3+

from three years & up

Growing independence and a wonderful way with words make your three-year-old a good-natured and fascinating companion. Eager to please, amuse, and help you, he loves making new friends, but he's still focused on his family. He is learning during every waking hour and drinking it all in: novelty and repetition, independence and closeness, the everyday and the unexpected. For a three-year-old, each day is a celebration.

1

house a bug

Make a bug-observation station for your young
naturalist by cutting a window in the side of
a round oatmeal container and taping a piece
of netting or screening over it. Gently place a
ladybug, beetle, or grasshopper inside for her
to examine. Talk about nurturing and
respecting tiny creatures before
releasing the insect near
the spot where you found it.

2

be backward

Kids love silliness, especially when an adult joins in. So declare "Backward Day," and help your child put on his clothes backward. Walk backward together and you won't know whether you're both coming or going!

3

tie-dye paper

Accordion-fold a piece of paper into a long strip, then accordion-fold that piece into a small square. Dilute different colors of nontoxic paint with water to the consistency of milk and pour each color into a cup in a muffin tray. Have your child dip the square's edges into different cups. Unfold the wet paper and allow to dry. See how the colors blend to make new shades?

4

make a bean mosaic

Pour an assortment of dried beans onto a tray and
put out cardboard, child-safe glue, and some
nontoxic markers. Invite your little one to draw
shapes and show her how to glue her beans
on the paper to fill in her design.

5

introduce the computer

Draw a large square divided into three rows and three
columns (like tic-tac-toe) on your computer. Teach your
child to use the "fill" or "paint" tool to claim a space
with his chosen color. Let him experiment with colors
and patterns. To play again, paint each square white.

6

look for animal homes

Read a book on wild animals' homes, then seek out
some in your backyard. Promising places to look include
tree branches for bird and squirrel nests, openings in
the ground for chipmunk and mole tunnels, and the
undersides of leaves for insect hideouts.

7

make time for rhymes

Play simple games to help your child understand—and
relish—the magic of rhyme. Ask her, "What rhymes
with *hat?*" "With *fun?*" When looking at a storybook
together, you might ask, "Can you find a picture of an
animal that rhymes with *big* on this page?"

8

choose the right trike

First tricycle? Make sure your easy rider's feet reach
the pedals comfortably. For safety, choose a steel frame
and make sure he wears a properly fitting helmet.
Spur your child's imagination by adding props to the
trike—today it's a spaceship, tomorrow a fire engine.

9

collage creatures

Cut body shapes of animals like sheep or ducks from heavy paper. Put out some crafts materials—nontoxic paints, crayons, wrapping paper, magazines, and macaroni—and invite your child to let her imagination run wild as she creates her very own menagerie.

10

walk like a duck

Use yellow craft foam to fashion ducky feet for your child to waddle around in. Cut out two foot shapes slightly larger than your child's feet. On each piece of foam, cut two horizontal slits 5 inches (13 cm) wide and 2 inches (5 cm) apart. Slide his feet through the slits to keep the foam in place. Time for a duck walk!

11

"when I'm feeling shy...
A puppet helps me
express myself and enjoy
telling you a story."

12

build in three dimensions

Help your child graduate from making flat paintings and drawings to creating multidimensional art. Give him materials like child-safe modeling clay to make simple sculptures of objects, people, and animals. Let him choose add-on materials for his masterpiece, such as assorted large child-safe buttons and pebbles.

13

listen to the night

On a night when your child is up past dark, dress her warmly or bundle her in a blanket and sit outside together. Hold her in your lap and ask her to close her eyes and listen. Does she hear crickets? Cars? An owl? Notice the different sounds and talk about the animals, vehicles, or people making them.

14

inspire make-believe

All kids love to pretend. Fuel the fun—and your child's imagination—by putting together (or adding to) a dress-up box of old costumes, clothes, hats, and jewelry. Don't offer lots of direction; just put the box out (especially when a friend is over to play) and see what kind of make-believe magic it inspires.

15

have a jam session

Using a recipe for no-cook jam, let your child mash
the berries and stir in the other ingredients. Enjoy the
homemade goodness by putting out child-safe utensils
so that he can make his own jam sandwich.

16

build skills

Build spatial relations, imagination, fine motor skills,
and the Empire State Building, all at the same time.
Offer your budding construction worker building toys:
blocks, logs, interlocking plastic bricks, stacking cups,
and empty shoe boxes. If possible, don't disturb her
little Taj Mahal. As time goes by, she might knock it
down—or create a whole town around it!

17

create a button bug

Read about insects together, or study some in your yard. Then invite your child to use buttons, nontoxic glue, and construction paper to make a bug of his own. Show him how to glue the buttons in a caterpillar shape with a larger button for the head. Have him add eyes and lots of tiny legs with a child-safe marker.

18

string a bird snack

Show your child how to thread O-shaped cereal onto strings (knot the ends to hold the pieces in place). Help her hang them on trees and shrubs for birds to snack on. Watch as the birds flock to the tasty treats!

19

find a rhyme

Why are so many nursery rhymes about losing things? Perhaps because three-year-olds spend a lot of time looking for things that have gone astray. Say this verse together and it might help you find that missing sock. For extra fun and silliness, personalize the rhyme by changing the first line to include your child's name and the item you're seeking.

Little Bo Peep has lost her sheep
And doesn't know where to find them.
Leave them alone and they'll come home,
Wagging their tails behind them.

20

open a doll clinic

Build your child's confidence and sense of empathy
by setting up a pretend doctor's office for his dolls and
plush animals. Outfit it with bandages, a toy syringe
(kids love giving "shots"), and a toy stethoscope for
checking furry heartbeats. He may feel a little braver
the next time he gets a boo-boo of his own.

21

watch feathered friends

Help your child use a simple bird guide to identify
some of the feathered visitors to your yard. Soon
they'll be as recognizable to her as old friends.
Then give her a disposable camera and let her take
pictures to make her own personal bird book.

22
plant sunflowers

It's a flower and a snack! In spring, help your child plant sunflowers and see how fast they reach for the sky. Create a photo book: take pictures when he plants the seeds, when the plants push through the soil, and when the stems grow to be taller than he is. Then help him paste the photos in a journal. When the flowers mature in late summer, let him harvest and eat the seeds. Put some out for the birds and squirrels to munch, too.

23

make a car quilt

Have your preschooler help you cut squares from some worn-out clothes. Use pieces of fabric associated with good, warm times, like strips cut from old pajamas or flannel shirts. Stitch them together and then add a solid fabric backing to make a super snuggly car blanket.

24

read alfresco

On a warm day, let your child pick out a special book to read in a shady spot in the yard, and make it cozy with a comfortable blanket that you and she can sprawl out on. Don't forget cool drinks, since reading can be thirsty work.

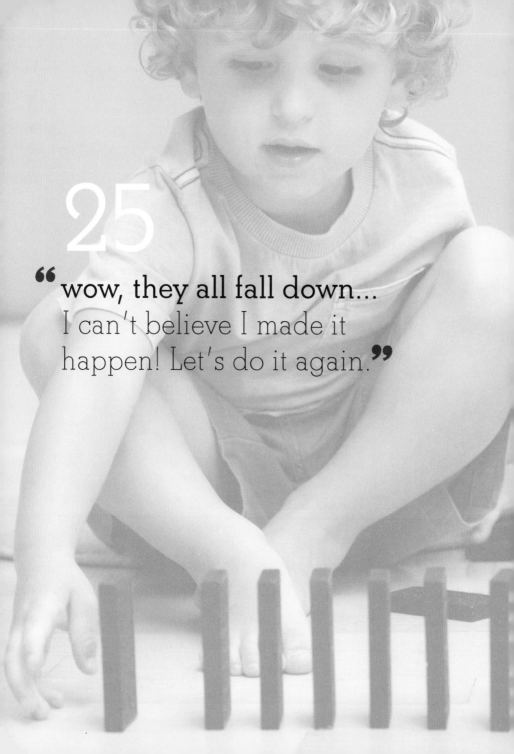

25

"**wow, they all fall down...** I can't believe I made it happen! Let's do it again."

26

fine-tune scissor skills

To help your child practice his scissor skills, encourage him to cut fringes along the edges of stiff paper. First, draw straight lines for him to cut along, then upgrade to more challenging wavy or dotted lines. Have him use kid-sized safety scissors and show him how holding a side of the paper makes cutting easier.

27

eat a rainbow

Go to the grocery store together and pick out lots of brightly colored (and nutrient-rich) fruits and veggies: scarlet beets, blue potatoes, emerald broccoli, purple grapes, and ruby strawberries. Once you've got the good stuff on hand, try together to eat as many different-colored foods as you can each day.

28

eat curds and whey

The origins of this old rhyme are murky, but the most popular theory is that it's about a little girl whose father, Dr. Thomas Muffet, wrote one of the first field guides to insects. If your little one wants to try out some curds and whey, go ahead and offer her some cottage cheese—but hold those creepy-crawly spiders!

Little Miss Muffet sat on a tuffet,
Eating her curds and whey.
Along came a spider,
Who sat down beside her,
And frightened Miss Muffet away!

29

read a bath-time story

Try reading to your child during his nighttime bath. If you pick a tale with a nautical theme, he might enjoy acting it out with his bath toys. By the time you've finished a story (or two), chances are your young mariner will be clean, calm, and halfway to dreamland.

30

get stuck on magnets

Teach your child about magnets by offering a selection to play with (always with supervision and a reminder to keep them away from computers and watches). Help her gather objects, ranging from large paper clips to crayons, and discover what sticks and what doesn't.

31

try out a trike course

In a flat, quiet space with no cars, use colored chalk to mark off straight and winding pathways, roundabouts, stop signs, and detours for your tricyclist to follow. Take a moment with him before he heads out onto the course and explain what all the different signs mean.

STOP

32

dig for dino eggs

Use self-drying, nontoxic clay to mold egg shapes
around small plastic dinosaurs, and have your
explorer hunt for them in a corner of the yard. Then
she can use her paleontology tools (spoons and toy
hammers) to uncover the "ancient" creatures inside.

33

watch a worm

Enough said. Just watch a worm with your little one.
Earthworms are easy to find in the garden or on the
sidewalk after a gentle rain. Watch them where they
are, or pick one up carefully and set it into his hand
(they're too fragile for a child to pick up). Talk about
how the worm feels. Cold? Warm? Slimy? If you
can't find worms, look for some ants instead.

34

be ambitious with sand

Three-year-olds are just coming into their sandbox glory days. The simple sensory joy of sand play is still with them (what feels better than running cool sand through your hands on a hot day?), but now their play is more purposeful: using tools and toys to pile, plow, dig, tunnel, and build. Sand toys don't have to be complicated. Spoons, shovels, scoops, cups, and water keep preschoolers busy in the sand for a long time. (Stay close by to supervise.)

35

learn an animal alphabet

Sit down with your child and read aloud a book that uses animals to illustrate the alphabet. Then have her name animals that start with *A, B,* and so on.

36

say what's in a name

Play a name game with your child. First, tell him his full name, and then have him tell you yours (your first and last names, not just "Mommy" or "Daddy"). This information is important in an emergency, but for now keep it light by also asking him the names of his siblings, dog, goldfish, and teddy bear. Challenge him gently: "Are you sure my name's Beth? I thought it was Mom. OK, if it's Beth, is it Beth Cupcake? No? You're right, it's Beth Johnson!"

37

stomp a song

Stomp together to this rhyme. Stomping helps
your child develop her sense of rhythm, which
in turn helps her develop her language skills.

I went to the animal fair,
The birds and the beasts were there.
The big baboon by the light of the moon,
Was combing his auburn hair.

The alligator and loon
Were strolling along the lagoon.
The loon gave a laugh to observe the giraffe
Try to unmask the raccoon.

38
freeze fruit

Here's a cool way to tempt your child with a healthy snack. Have him arrange favorite fruits in an ice cube tray and freeze them. Once the treats are frozen, enjoy them or store in plastic bags for later. Apple chunks, blueberries, pitted cherries—so many options!

39
overcome obstacles

Challenge your budding gymnast by setting up an impromptu obstacle course where she can tumble over pillows, crawl under the table, and jump off a bottom step. Give her plenty of encouragement and support, and always stay close at hand to supervise.

40

create a beach collage

Mark a recent outing—or conjure up the shore when summer or the sea is far away—with a do-it-yourself beach. Invite your child to decorate sturdy cardboard with hand-collected or store-bought shells and sand. He can paint the surf or make it from blue paper.

41

bake granola

Have your child mix 4 cups (1 l) of raw oats in a bowl with a small amount of any of these: wheat germ, sunflower seeds, sesame seeds, raisins, chopped dried fruit, coconut flakes. Ask her to drizzle the mixture with honey and stir in a big spoonful of canola oil. Bake on a cookie sheet at 325°F (160°C), stirring occasionally (an adult job), for 20 minutes or until golden.

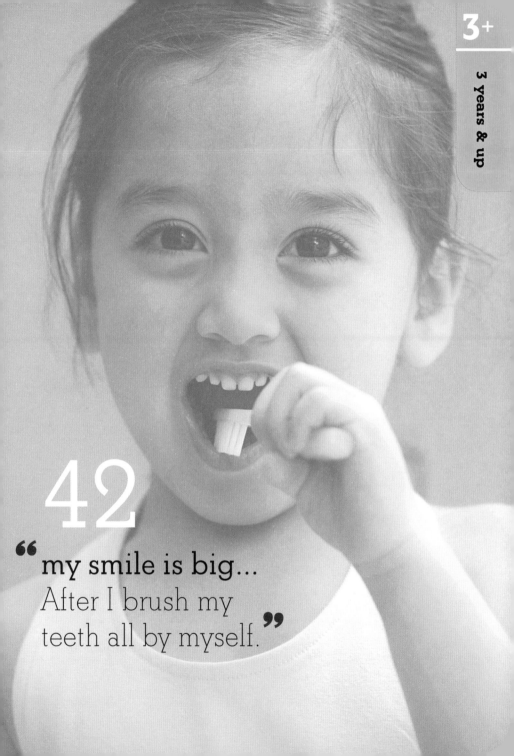

42

" my smile is big...
After I brush my
teeth all by myself. "

43

nurture fresh herbs

Help your child plant herb seedlings in three broad clay pots about 4 inches (10 cm) deep. Thyme, dill, and oregano are child-friendly flavors, or he might like to try some mint. Set the pots on a moderately sunny windowsill and help your little gardener keep the soil moist. As the plants grow, he can pinch off leaves to enhance whatever you're having for dinner.

44

cultivate friendships

Invite your preschooler's friends over to play. To encourage cooperative play, balance free time with special activities, such as baking cookies, building a city out of blocks, or washing the dog.

45

feed the birds

Make a winter treat for the birds by helping your child combine a cup each of peanut butter, cornmeal, raisins, chopped apples, and birdseed in a large bowl. Have her mix the ingredients and form the mixture into a ball, tie it up in a plastic mesh bag (the kind potatoes come in), and hang it outside for the birds.

46

have a colorful day

Have your child pick a color theme for the day. Say it's purple: he might wear a purple T-shirt and paint a picture of grapes. Then read Crockett Johnson's *Harold and the Purple Crayon* together.

47

disguise math

Slip a little math into daily activities. Ask your child to count out three eggs to help you make a cake or, while at the beach, to pour sand into a cup until it's half full. As she gets better at simple problems, casually introduce harder ones: "Andy and Amy are coming over, so we'll need a plum for each of you to snack on. How many plums do we need to buy at the store?"

48

admire pussy willows

In late winter or early spring, take your child
to a wooded area or a garden shop to look
for fuzzy pussy-willow branches. Bring the
branches home and put them in a vase for
him to examine. They may even inspire him to
make some art: give him paper and nontoxic
brown paint to draw the stems. When the
paint is dry, have him add puffs by dipping
a fingertip or a cotton swab in gray paint
and pressing it against a stem.

49

prep for a plane ride

Pack paper, crayons, stickers, a favorite soft toy, finger puppets, and books in a cabin-sized (and child-sized) bag. Add raisins, crackers, and something chewy like a rolled fruit snack to ease "popping" ears for your little voyager. If you're traveling light, consider boarding later. That way she'll have more time to explore the airport and shake all of her wiggles out.

50

go from mineral to animal

Take a field trip together and hunt for some interesting rocks—ones that are shiny, ridged, or unusually colored. Let your child wash and dry his rocks and set him up with art supplies (such as nontoxic paint and glue, yarn, and buttons) to make zany animals.

51

chart the weather

Cover a heavy piece of cardboard with blue and green felt to resemble the grass and the sky. Purchase or make felt cutouts in shapes that represent the sun, white and gray clouds, raindrops, snowflakes, and lightning. Have your child mirror the day's weather by adding those shapes to her grass and sky canvas.

52

dip a pretzel

Put out a small bowl of room-temperature almond
butter or cream cheese and a plate of raisins, chopped
dates, or coconut flakes (or a mix of all three). Teach
your little gourmet how to dip one end of a fat pretzel
rod into the bowl, and then dab it onto the plate of
dried fruit to create a new taste sensation!

53

pack a lunch

Invite your child to decorate plain paper lunch bags
using stamps, stickers, and markers. Or let him pick
clip-art images from a computer graphics program
and print them onto white paper bags (check your
printer manual for the right settings). Then have him
help you pack his lunch in a personalized bag.

54

sing a verse

Sing this song once to your child and
then make up some new verses together.

Down by the bay,
Where the watermelons grow,
Back to my home,
I dare not go,
For if I do,
My mother will say,
"Did you ever see a bear,
Combing his hair,
Down by the bay?"
"Did you ever see a moose,
Kissing a goose,
Down by the bay?"

55

" **with my own tools...**
I can help you clean up
around the house. It makes
me feel grown-up. "

56

pick your own

Visit a pick-your-own farm with your child. Blueberries and apples are especially easy to pick. Keep the visit short, allow a little snacking, and let her carry her part of the harvest to the weighing stand. At home, read a book about picking fruit together, like *Blueberries for Sal* by Robert McCloskey, and talk about your outing.

57

improve trail mix

Have your pint-sized explorer make trail mix by enhancing granola. Add scoops of dried cherries or pineapple, chopped dates, banana chips, almonds, yogurt-covered raisins, sunflower seeds, shelled pistachios, or cereal. Then hit the trails!

58

care for pets

A three-year-old is big enough to be a good friend to cats, dogs, mice, and whatever else shares your home. Have your little one feed the family pets; fill their water bowls; brush and groom them; help wipe up their paw prints or spills; and even help train them, offering small food rewards when they follow instructions. There's no one like a preschooler to have the energy to run and play with a puppy.

59

shadow a poet

Help your child find his shadow, then read
this Robert Louis Stevenson poem together.

*I have a little shadow that
goes in and out with me,
And what can be the use of
him is more than I can see.
He is very, very like me from
the heels up to the head;
And I see him jump before me,
when I jump into my bed.*

*The funniest thing about him
is the way he likes to grow—
Not at all like proper children,
which is always very slow;
For he sometimes shoots up
taller like an India-rubber ball,
And he sometimes gets so
little that there's none of him at all.*

60
sort the laundry

Liven up laundry day by turning a household chore into a fun sorting game. Enlist your preschooler to match up clean socks and sort out the big T-shirts from the little ones. Not only will he relish the chance to help you, but he'll also learn about matching sizes, colors, and patterns.

61
pack a bag for quiet time

Fill a small bag with quiet amusements that can pass the time in best-behavior situations, like a sibling's school concert. Small plush toys, finger puppets, rag dolls, and cloth books are good choices. Reinforce the "silent" theme by reserving the bag just for those occasions that require quiet.

62

discover color

Most preschoolers know their basic colors, but there's more than one shade of blue, right? Demonstrate sorting the crayons from a large box into different groups—all the blues, all the greens, and all the pinks, for instance—and talk about the color names with your budding artist. As you go through the day, encourage him to make up color names like rubber-duck yellow, marmalade orange, and beach-ball red.

63

get a blast from the past

Take your child's baby toys out of storage. Even though she's outgrown them as regular playthings, she'll be delighted by a brief reunion with her rattles, squeak toys, simple books, and musical shakers.

64

muddy a pig

Cut a large piece of paper into the shape of a pig.
Have your child draw on a face, then dab on some
brown nontoxic paint "mud" with a clean sponge.
When the project's done, chances are the pig won't
be the only one artistically smeared with paint!

65

visit a photo booth

Head to a photo booth together and pose for some
pictures. Go for a different mood in each picture: silly,
serious, or sleepy, for instance. Display the photo strip
on the fridge or in your child's room. Or laminate it,
punch a hole in the top, and loop a ribbon through
the hole to make a bookmark your child will treasure.

66

meet animals

A petting zoo or farm open to the public may be more appealing to your brave three-year-old than it was when he was younger. Talk about what kinds of animals you see there and what they like to eat. Any time your child is around animals, especially unfamiliar ones, supervise closely, and always ask the staff or owner of the animals whether it's safe to touch them. Demonstrate for him how to move quietly and slowly to make the animals comfortable. And be sure you both wash your hands afterward.

67

do a blind fruit-tasting

When you're making a fruit salad, invite your child
to join you and turn food prep into a game. Have her
close her eyes and guess which fruit you just popped
into her mouth. Talk about taste and texture. Was it
tart like an apple? Or soft like a banana?

68

twist pipe dreams

Set your child up with a bunch of pipe cleaners in
different thicknesses, lengths, and colors. Watch his
creativity soar as he twists them into sculptures. If
he wants to branch out into mixed media, give him
materials such as pom-poms, yarn, and buttons to
embellish his fanciful pipe-cleaner creations.

69

play with letters

Give your bathing buddy foam letters to float in the bathtub. Show her how to press the wet letters onto the side of the tub or the wall. You can get in some ABC practice or just let her play with the letters and help her feel comfortable with the alphabet.

70

see what temperature can do

If it's literally freezing out, fill a cake pan two-thirds full of water. Ask your child to gather evergreen sprigs or other greenery and lay them in the pan. Make a loop of twine and submerge half of it in the water. Leave the pan outside until the water freezes, then turn the ice out of the pan and hang it outside. If it's warm out, use your freezer, then later watch the artwork melt.

71

capture the routine

Talk with your child about a typical day for him, then help him create a "day in the life" book with photos or drawings showing him in pursuits like eating breakfast or playing with friends. It will become a treasured keepsake he'll love to look at now and in the years to come (and it makes a great gift for relatives, too).

72

make an impression

Sit with your child and together form nontoxic, self-drying clay into a walnut-sized ball and flatten it. Have her press a leaf, a shell, or an acorn into the clay to make an impression, then peel the clay off. Use a drinking straw to poke a hole near the clay's edge. Let the clay dry before adding a string to make a necklace.

73

"watch me hop...
I don't even need
you to hold my
hand while I jump
on one foot!**"**

74

befriend bats

Read about bats in *Stella Luna,* noting how they hunt using their own radar system and eat hundreds of insects a day. Then scan the sky at dusk for the nighttime flyers. Chat about other fascinating, useful, but not-so-cuddly animals, like bees and worms. Explain that each animal has an important job to do, like making honey or aerating the soil, and that most won't bother us if we don't bother them.

75

stretch yourselves

Kids love moving and imitating what you do, so expand your yoga repertoire together. Look at a book or a DVD that has lots of poses—kids especially love the Downward-Facing Dog—or take a class together. Then spread out a mat or towel and practice at home.

76

puzzle out a frame

Recycle a puzzle with missing pieces by using the remaining pieces to get crafty. Help your child glue them onto a cardboard picture frame (one you bought or one you cut out yourself). When the glue is dry, your young artist might want to embellish the frame with nontoxic poster paint, glitter, buttons, or other trims and use it to frame a photo or drawing.

77

pilot a plane

Introduce your preschooler to paper airplanes. First, invite her to use crayons or nontoxic markers to color her craft. Then show her how to fold it into an airplane shape and let it fly. Build her imagination and sense of geography by talking about the places she might want to visit in a real plane someday.

78

make yarn art

Outfit your child with leftover yarn of different colors, textures, and lengths. Then give him a glue stick, paper, and other artistic fodder like buttons or dried pasta shapes so he can create vibrant 3-D collages.

79

go on a scavenger hunt

Sit down with your child and come up with
a scavenger hunt list (using both words and
pictures) of things you might find in the woods
or a park. The list might include a Y-shaped
twig, an acorn, a white stone, a ladybug, and a
bird's nest. Then take a hike to find them. On
another day, you might make a list of things
to hunt for in town. See if your little scavenger
can find things like a planter full of flowers, a
clock, a place to sit outside, and a fountain.

80

count out flapjacks

Whip up a stack of five silver-dollar pancakes. When they've cooled, give your child blueberries and invite her to use them to "number" each flapjack, poking one berry into the top of the first one, two into the second one, and so on. Then ask her to make a tough decision—will she start eating the pancakes in order from one to five, or begin at five and work backward?

81

play tug-of-war

Hand your child a long piece of rope, a thin blanket, or scarves tied tightly together. Pull gently on your end while he tugs back, building his strength and confidence. Keep the game lighthearted by letting him tug you off balance and lead you around.

82

pot a pineapple

Teach your child about nature and encourage a green thumb. Twist or cut off the stalk of leaves from the top of a pineapple (adult job). Have her set the stalk in water for a few days until you see roots, and then plant the seedling in potting soil, watering it when the soil dries out. She'll soon have a sprouting pineapple tree!

83

have a Q&A

Divert your child—and promote logical thinking—by asking him fun questions about animals and nature. For instance, you might ask, "What has four legs and moos?" or "What animal hops and says 'ribbit'?"

84

bring out a surprise

Inevitably, your child will have days when she's too sick to go out, but well enough to enjoy quiet indoor activities—and being fussed over a little. For those days, keep a box or basket tucked away that has some special treats to lift your little patient's spirits. This might include a set of temporary tattoos, some fresh modeling clay, a new water bottle (great for encouraging her to drink enough liquids), and a book of simple puzzles, pictures to color, or easy mazes. (If she's not ready to put pen to paper, she can use her finger to trace her way out of mazes.)

85

swim for safety

Head out to the pool for some fun and exercise.
If you haven't already introduced your little one to
swimming, three is a great age to do so (and if you
live near a pool or a naturally occurring body of water,
it's an essential part of keeping him safe). If you're
not a strong swimmer yourself, you might start by
taking a parent-child swim class together. Remember
that even after taking swim classes, no child should
ever be left unattended near water.

86

"let me try new foods
like kiwifruit…
I may even like it
enough to eat more
than just one bite."

87

get a feel for letters

Cut the letters of your child's first name out of
sandpaper. Invite her to trace the tactile shapes with
her finger, building her familiarity with the alphabet
and putting her on the road to spelling her name.

88

paint postcards

Buy stiff watercolor paper at an art store and cut it into
postcard-sized pieces. Show your young artist how to
brush the paper lightly with water, then have him dab
a brush dipped in nontoxic paint onto the paper. This
wet-on-wet technique can produce effects that look
just like sunsets, shadows, or reflections. When his
masterpieces are dry, display them—or add addresses
and stamps and mail them to friends and family.

89
chart growth

Have your child help you make a growth chart. Roll out a long piece of paper and paint a tree, a flower, or a vine. Then measure her against the paper and add a leaf, a bloom, or a butterfly to mark her height. Note the date and your child's age at the mark, too.

90
make it abstract

Pieces of string dragged through nontoxic tempera paint can be used to make great abstract art. Have your little artist dip a string into paint, and then drop the string onto a piece of paper on a washable floor. He can then pick up the string and repeat the process—or use a new piece of string dipped in another color—until he decides his artwork is finished.

91

clap for joy

Preschoolers love happy, active songs—and
this one fits the bill perfectly.

*If you're happy and you know it,
Clap your hands.*

clap clap

*If you're happy and you know it,
Clap your hands.*

clap clap

*If you're happy and you know it,
Then your face will surely show it.
If you're happy and you know it,
Clap your hands.*

clap clap

For the next verses, your child can stamp her
feet, shout "hurray!"—or do all three.

92

count in two languages

Your preschooler can hone his math and language
skills with this fun bilingual counting chant.

Uno, dos, y tres,
Cuatro, cinco, seis.
Siete, ocho, nueve,
Cuento hasta diez.
La la la la la. La la la la la,

One, two, and three,
Four, five, and six.
Seven, eight, and nine,
I count to ten.
La la la la la. La la la la la.

93

catch a cookie

Adventurous three-year-olds admire the star of *The Gingerbread Man:* the cookie who jumped out of the oven and ran from everyone who tried to catch him. Bake some gingerbread folks together, decorating them with raisins or chocolate chips. After the cookies cool, add frosting touches such as buttons and bows. Then enjoy one with your child while you read the story together. Keep an eye on your gingerbread people so they don't run off while you're reading!

94

play with words

Have some fun with language by indulging in silly
rhymes and alliteration. Ask your child to "put on
your boat...I mean your goat...no, your coat." Declare
your child's lunch "tasty tuna to tempt tastebuds."
She'll giggle at your goofiness—and will start thinking
about words (and playing with them) on her own.

95

set up an oatmeal bar

If your child likes oatmeal or other hot cereals, it's
easy to dish up a healthy breakfast. If things start
feeling routine, surprise him with a breakfast buffet.
Set out tiny bowls of mix-ins: raisins, dried cranberries,
sliced almonds or walnut pieces, banana slices, and
sunflower seeds are healthy and delicious options.

96

tell fish tales

Read some books on fish and marine life together,
then take a trip to an aquarium or a pet shop. Look at
as many marine animals as you can, talk about them
with your child, and pick out your favorites. Does she
favor colorful fish, odd-looking crabs, or funny frogs?
Ask her which animal she'd like to be, and why.

97

watch out for snowballs

Show your child how to roll balls of snow to make snow people—or snow dogs, cats, or snakes—and decorate them with carrots, twigs, and stones. He can probably trudge through the snow pretty steadily now, as long as it's not too deep, but do keep an eye on him. Be careful—you may find he can pack some pretty good snowballs now, too. No snow where you live? Make some with soap flakes and water.

98

string a bead or two

Your child can handle small beads and fine string now, and will love novelties such as ribbon, alphabet beads for spelling her name, or photosensitive beads that go from white to colored in sunlight and fade indoors.

99

dot ladybugs

Set your child up with some precut red circles and nontoxic washable markers, and help him transform the circles into ladybugs. He can add more buggy features, if he likes, such as pipe-cleaner antennae.

100

bake pretzels

Help your child roll whole-grain bread dough into long snakes, then bend them into pretzel shapes. (Remember, not all pretzels look alike—make snails, geometric shapes, letters, or just twist them.) Place them on a baking sheet and brush with a little water, then sprinkle with salt. Bake at 375°F (190°C) for 12 minutes or until golden. Let them cool before munching.

101

assist animals

Three-year-olds are too young to volunteer, but your
little one can help furry friends by gathering blankets
or cat-food coupons for an animal shelter or by feeding
a vacationing neighbor's dog with you. She'll love
nurturing animals—and Fido will relish the company!

102

catch sunshine in a pitcher

Make caffeine-free iced tea as a treat on a hot day, but
let your child—and the sun—do all the work. Have him
unwrap a couple of tea bags (herbal teas work, too) and
drop them in a pitcher of water. Cover the pitcher with
plastic wrap, then have him place it in a sunny spot
outdoors. Let the tea brew for a few hours, checking
on it until it's the strength you like. Serve with ice.

103

"watch those bubbles fly... And catch them as they float by."

104

swing, swing, swing

At the park, choose a swing with a plastic or rubber seat and help your child get pumping. To teach her how to keep the swing in motion, gently guide her legs so that she's up in the air, then let go and have her bend them on the way back. Then sit on a swing beside her and demonstrate as you swing side by side.

105

sing a prairie song

Your young cowpoke will enjoy "Home on the Range."

Oh, give me a home where the buffalo roam,
Where the deer and the antelope play.
Where seldom is heard a discouraging word,
And the skies are not cloudy all day.

Home, home on the range,
Where the deer and the antelope play.
Where seldom is heard a discouraging word,
And the skies are not cloudy all day.

106

try an inkblot test

Have your child fold a sheet of paper in half, then unfold it and drop a few blobs of paint in different colors on one half of the inside. Then help him refold the paper, pressing with his hand. When he opens it up again, ask him what he sees in the picture.

107

eat like a bunny

Here's a surefire way to instill a love of healthy food in your child. Put out a plate of raw vegetables, and help your little one make a variety of dips using simple recipes. Explain that veggies are a bunny's favorite delicacy—and watch them disappear!

108

seek out sequels

Fuel your little bookworm's enthusiasm for reading
by looking for sequels featuring some of her favorite
characters, like the Cat in the Hat, Rainbow Fish, or
Angelina Ballerina. The familiar characters will feel
like old friends, and chances are she'll be eager
to continue on to the next book in the series.

109

make a fluffy friend

Draw the outline of a sheep with white chalk
on a piece of black construction paper. Give
your child a bag of cotton balls and nontoxic
glue, and see how woolly the sheep can become.
If he leaves the face uncovered, he can use
the chalk to add eyes, a nose, and a mouth.

110

take a chalkboard to go

Cover the top of a hinged-lid box (like a lunch box)
with chalkboard paint from a crafts store. Help your
child pack the box with colored chalks and an eraser,
and she'll have a portable drawing center.

111

piece a paper quilt

Talk with your child about how people make quilts
from fabric scraps. Then have him use nontoxic glue
to stick colored construction-paper squares on a larger
piece of paper to create his own design. Display
his artwork by hanging a string across a wall and
fastening his paper quilt to it with clothespins.

112

get stamping

Sit your child down with some stamps (or just use leftover puzzle pieces or foam bath letters and shapes). Show her how to press them into a pad of nontoxic, washable ink or nontoxic paint and stamp letter designs or her initials on paper.

113

draw a reflection

Now that your child's getting older, he's ready to try drawing from life—and what better model than himself? Invite him to stand in front of a full-length mirror, study his reflection, then sit down and draw what he saw. He can come back to the mirror any time he wants to refresh his memory or check a new detail.

114

have a sponge toss

Cool off on a hot day by tossing a large sponge soaked in cold water back and forth between you. Or have your child soak the sponge and toss it high in the air before catching it again.

115

layer nachos

Nachos are kid-pleasers because children can put what they like on them. Have your child help you layer tortilla chips and shredded cheese on a plate. Then invite her to add her favorite nacho fixings: cooked shredded chicken or ground beef, black beans, or salsa. Microwave on low until the cheese melts, then let the nachos cool a bit before adding sour cream or guacamole, if desired. Now munch away!

116

grow beans

After the frosts, help your child poke
four or five tall bamboo garden stakes
into the ground in your yard, arranged
in a circle about 3 feet (1 m) across.
Use garden twine to gather and tie the
tops of the stakes together, then plant
a bean seed at the base of each stake.
As the beanstalks grow, show him how
to twine them around the stakes. Once
they're tall and lush, usher your little
one into his very own bean teepee and
read *Jack and the Beanstalk* together.

117

"red foot,
green foot...
I can make art
lots of ways—even
with my feet!"

118

climb like a spider

Help your three-year-old burn off some of her
excess energy by inviting her to imitate different
insects and animals. Spider stretches are a good
way to start: ask her to lie on her back with
her arms and legs in the air. Then have her
work her limbs superfast, like a spider
climbing a thread up to the center of its web.

119

paint a song

Is your petit Picasso looking for inspiration?
Try dancing and singing a favorite song together.
Talk about how the song makes him feel and suggest
he try his hand at illustrating those feelings.

120

collage a shape

Reinforce your child's ability to recognize and name shapes by having her make a picture entirely out of variations of a single shape—say, squares or triangles. First, get her familiar with the shape. Have her help you cut its form out in different sizes from various colors of construction paper, wrapping paper, magazines, newspapers, or even fabric. Then help her use nontoxic glue to collage a person, an animal, or any abstract pattern. Can she use two brown triangles to make a friend's pigtails? How about kitty's ears?

121

camp in your yard

Have a family campout in the backyard, either in
a tent or under the open sky in sleeping bags spread
out on blankets. Roast hot dogs and marshmallows
over the grill, tell stories by flashlight, and then
snuggle down to sleep. If it gets cold or the night
noises keep you awake, finish the night indoors. No
yard? Just set up a campout in your living room!

4+

from four years & up

Your four-year-old is remarkably competent at dealing with the world. Proud of her rich vocabulary and equipped with a playful sense of humor, she may be feisty at times. On the other hand, four-year-olds tend to get frustrated less often than younger kids, since they can better understand how things work, including the reasons why they can't always have their way. Add in well-developed fine and gross motor skills, and your four-year-old is ready to take on the world—but she still wants you to be there beside her to join in the fun.

122

make a box car

A large cardboard box and some nontoxic markers are all your child needs to make a vehicle all his own. Be sure to remove any staples, then help him add accessories like paper-plate wheels and headlights made from plastic cups. Throw in a pillow—and maybe a small trailer for a stuffed animal—and he's ready to hit the road.

123

tote a tic-tac-toe

Buy a whiteboard or make a portable tic-tac-toe set
by having your child draw a tic-tac-toe board on stiff
cardboard, laminating it at a copy shop, punching a
hole in a corner, and using string to tie on an erasable
marker. After she plays a match with a friend in the
car, at the park, or wherever she happens to be, clear
the board with a tissue so it's ready for the next round.

124

clean up by color

Big mess in your child's room? Turn cleanup into
a sorting game by having him tidy up according to
color. For instance, he might put away all the red
things, then the brown ones—then blue, then green,
then white—until everything's in its place again.

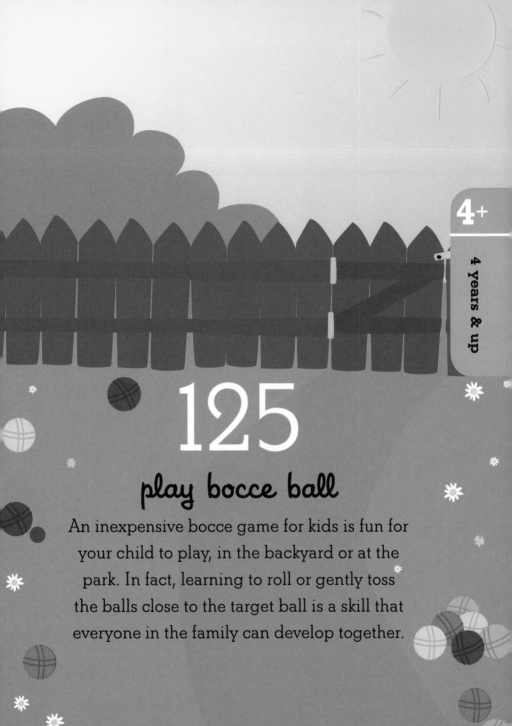

125

play bocce ball

An inexpensive bocce game for kids is fun for your child to play, in the backyard or at the park. In fact, learning to roll or gently toss the balls close to the target ball is a skill that everyone in the family can develop together.

126

study syllables

Teach your budding linguist about the building blocks of language by having her count out the syllables in words with hand claps. Make it more fun by putting on some music she loves and having her clap out the syllables of familiar lyrics.

127

sculpt sand

Pick up sand in an array of colors at a crafts shop. Set your child up with the sand; clean, empty baby food jars (with the labels removed); and a spoon so he can fill the jars with layers of sand in different colors to make multihued sculptures.

128

be calculating

Teach your child to use a calculator (one with large buttons makes things easier for little fingers). Playing with the calculator builds coordination. Plus, it sparks interest in numbers and basic adding and subtracting.

4+

4 years & up

129

complete a cookout

Make banana splits on the outdoor grill or in the oven. Slit the curved side of a banana (with the peel on) and let your child stuff the opening with mini marshmallows and chocolate chips. Wrap the banana in two layers of foil and heat it (adults only) for a few minutes on each side. Eat with a spoon when cool.

130

float a boat

Invite your youngster to use crayons to color a piece of paper however she desires, then help her fold the paper into a simple boat to float in the bathtub or wading pool. The wax from the crayons will help the craft stay afloat. (Always supervise water play.)

131

draw freehand

Teach your child how to make a looping, squiggly, freehand line in black crayon on white paper without raising the crayon, finishing so the line ends where it began. Encourage your young illustrator to use all the crayons in the box to fill in his drawing.

132

tweak humpty dumpty

As you and your child make eggs together, recite this rhyme—a twist on the beloved nursery classic.

Humpty Dumpty sat on the wall.
Humpty Dumpty had a great fall.
All the king's horses and all the king's men
Had scrambled eggs for breakfast again!

4+

4 years & up

133

read true tales

Make sure your preschooler's library includes not just storybooks but also simple nonfiction books. Preschoolers love paging through books about animals, transportation, or dinosaurs, as well as how-to books featuring games, crafts, or cooking.

134

"I'm helping the world... I cut the plastic rings on soda cans so animals don't get caught in them.**"**

135

watch history come alive

Visit a living history museum where actors recreate
life from a different time or culture. Before you go,
read about the period being depicted, and call to
find out when there are hands-on activities for visitors,
such as turning a butter churn or trying out foods
that were popular during the period portrayed.

136

bead a bookmark

Help your child cut a foot-long (about 30 cm) piece
of hemp or linen cord (available at crafts or beading
stores). Tie a double knot, one that's too big for a
bead to slip over, about 3 inches (8 cm) from each
end. Have your child string a few beads at each end,
then tie new knots to hold the beads in place.

137

frame your pet

Create a frame for a picture of your family pet by cutting a small rectangle from the center of a larger rectangle of heavy cardboard. Help your child coat the frame with clear-drying, nontoxic crafts glue. While it's wet, have her attach dog biscuits, dry cat treats, or a layer of birdseed, matching the treat to the pet. Then have her give the pet food a coat of glue to preserve it (and so it no longer tempts your pet). When dry, glue in your pet's photo, attach a magnet to the back, and display your child's handiwork on the refrigerator.

138

let the reading begin!

Your four-year-old may be ready for picture books with more text, and may even start picking out a few familiar words while you're reading to him. Encourage language pattern recognition by offering him stories that have similar themes or repeat key words.

139

draw self-portraits

A great way to find out how your child sees herself is to ask her to make a few pictures: a portrait of her face, a drawing that shows her body, and a picture of herself doing something she loves. Label them with the date and store in a folder or album. Next year, ask her to make more pictures. If she compares them with the older drawings, she'll see how much she's grown.

140

hit the trail

A hike in the woods (or through local streets) is a full-scale family adventure. Set a comfortable pace for your child, bring bottles of water and light snacks, and take time to observe the plants and animals (or notable buildings and landmarks) you encounter along the way. Don't try to cover more ground than your child can handle—and make sure you all save some energy for the return trip!

141

sing a farming song

This song is a way to get your child thinking about nature and where his food comes from. Repeat the first verse after the second and third ones.

Oats and peas and barley grow,
Oats and peas and barley grow.
Do you or I or anyone know
How oats and peas and barley grow?

First the farmer sows his seed,
Stands up tall and takes his ease.
He stamps his foot and claps his hands,
And turns around to view his lands.

Last the farmer harvests his seed,
Stands up tall and takes his ease.
He stamps his foot and claps his hands,
And turns around to view his lands.

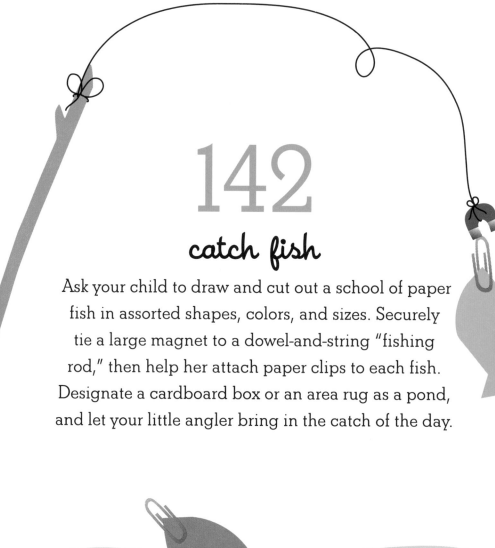

142

catch fish

Ask your child to draw and cut out a school of paper fish in assorted shapes, colors, and sizes. Securely tie a large magnet to a dowel-and-string "fishing rod," then help her attach paper clips to each fish. Designate a cardboard box or an area rug as a pond, and let your little angler bring in the catch of the day.

143
bake "clay" dough

Have your child shape store-bought or homemade bread dough as if it were clay, making whatever he fancies: a snake with a pointed tongue, or a lion with a mane of small strips. Bake at 375°F (190°C) until brown. When it's cool, he can eat his creation.

144
put together a first-aid kit

Teach your little one about being prepared by assembling a family first-aid kit together. Fill a watertight plastic box with antibiotic ointment, anti-itch cream, tweezers, cloth tape, gauze pads, and antiseptic wipes. Add a plush toy to soothe your little patient—maybe a "boo-boo bear." She can even practice first aid on the toy.

145

put on a show

Most preschoolers would agree with Shakespeare: the play's the thing. Encourage your aspiring dramatist to act out a favorite story with siblings or friends by offering old clothes for costumes and a clear space for a stage (since all the world's a stage, right?). Then sit back and enjoy the show.

146

start a scrapbook

Give your child a simple scrapbook (a binder with plastic sleeves will do nicely) for collecting whatever mementos mean the most to him, be they birthday greetings, vacation postcards, movie ticket stubs, blue ribbons from playing sports, pressed flowers, autumn leaves, or favorite photos.

147

play badminton

Set up a badminton game. The shuttlecocks ("birdies" to your child) are safe and lightweight, and she'll be thrilled every time one clears the net. If playing the game is still too challenging for your preschooler, just bouncing the shuttlecocks up and down on the rackets helps to develop coordination.

4+

4 years & up

148

hurry spring along

On a day when the temperature's above freezing, cut some forsythia branches that are 2 to 3 feet (about 60 to 90 cm) long and put them in a bucket of warm water for an hour. Transfer them to a vase of room-temperature water, and in a few days you'll be rewarded with golden blossoms—indoors!

149

outfit your young explorer

Have your child help you cut off the legs from a pair of his outgrown jeans or khakis. Help him sew the leg openings closed, tie a cord to the belt loops on the right and left sides to make a shoulder strap, and he's got an explorer's bag. Stock it with a compass, a magnifying glass, a pen, a notebook, a snack, a water bottle, and a kids' portable field guide. Then give him a good dose of sunscreen and a hat to keep the sun out of his eyes, and he'll be all set to explore the world's remote corners—or at least the backyard.

150

"look at my necklace...
I made it from a
shell that I found
at the beach."

151

personalize pet bowls

Let your child use nontoxic paint pens from a crafts store to decorate his cat's or dog's plastic food and water dishes with some animal-friendly illustrations.

152

give flowers

May Day (May 1) is the traditional day for leaving surprise nosegays of flowers at people's doors, but it's a charming idea for any day. Help your child to gather and tie a tiny bouquet and attach a note with a friendly message. Then play lookout while she tiptoes up to leave it on a neighbor's doorstep before making a quiet getaway (well, except for the giggles).

153

look for a four-leaf clover

Only one out of every 10,000 or so clovers has
four leaves instead of the standard-issue three, but
finding the time to search for one together on
a beautiful day is already pretty lucky.

154

share a joke

Sharpen your child's appreciation for verbal wit—and
tickle his funny bone—by sharing a joke like this one.

Knock, knock!
Who's there?
Olive.
Olive who?
Olive YOU!

155

fill a book

Fold five sheets of letter-sized paper in half, tuck them inside a folded sheet of construction paper, and staple the "spine" edge to give your child a blank book to fill with drawings, letter-writing practice, tic-tac-toe games, or a story that you make up together and your child illustrates.

156

dig those rocks

Even if your child's too young to know her igneous from her sedimentary, rock collecting is a great hobby for preschoolers. Whether she specializes in mica chips, collects colored pebbles, or brings a special stone home from every vacation, she'll appreciate having a shelf or box to house her collection.

157

ride a pony

A four-year-old is mature and coordinated enough to ride a pony in well-supervised situations. At birthday parties and fairs, an adult should hold the animal's lead and walk beside the riding child, with the pony going no faster than a walk. At a riding school, safety precautions should include a helmet for every child and wood chips or mulch to pad the ground underneath. Teach your young equestrian to approach the pony slowly and calmly, and never to walk or stand behind a pony or horse. And pony treats like carrots should be offered only with the handler's supervision.

4+

4 years & up

158

have fun in the car

When you're on a road trip, give your child a list (with small pictures, if needed) of items to look for: a cow, a bus, a barn, a lake, a stop sign, and so on. Have her cross off each item as she spots it. (If two children are playing, each child can count the items on his or her side of the car.) Tip: always have a new list ready to go.

159

host an almost-sleepover

Let your child invite a friend or two (and their plush animal buddies) to visit in their pajamas one evening. After supper and a little playtime, settle everyone down in their sleeping bags to hear a story. Arrange for your guests' parents to pick them up afterward so they can sleep soundly in their own beds.

4+

4 years & up

160

grow catnip

Catnip seeds, a flowerpot 8 inches (20 cm) across, potting soil, and a sunny spot on a counter are all your child needs to grow cat treats. Once the seeds sprout (about two weeks after planting), snipping off bits to treat your cat will make the plant grow even bushier.

161

work together

Preschoolers love helping out, so ask yours to assist you with chores whenever possible. Get him a child-sized broom, for instance, and put him to work!

162

go fish

Deal out 14 cards: seven for you and seven for your child. Take turns asking for a specific value from each other's hand ("Have any threes?"). The player asked the question must surrender all such cards. If she doesn't have any, her response is "Go fish." The other player then draws a card from the deck. If that yields a pair, the player lays down the matching cards and asks again. If not, the next player asks for a card. The first player to pair up all the cards in her hand wins.

163

create giant bubbles

4+

4 years & up

Join your child in making giant bubbles on a sunny day. Cut a straw in half crosswise, thread a yard (about 1 m) of string through the pieces, and knot the ends. Head outside and dip the straw pieces and string into a bowl or pan of store-bought bubble solution. Holding the pieces of the straw apart, wave them gently to create huge bubbles. Now let your child try it. Once he gets the hang of it, he won't want to stop!

164

make a family tree

Have your budding genealogist draw a tree with several branches. Cut out circles from another piece of paper, have her draw family members on them, then help her use nontoxic glue to attach them to the tree.

165

"wow...
I see amazing things
when I look through
a magnifying glass.**"**

166

sing your own song

Kids love songs that have their name or something related to them in the music. With your child, make up verses to a favorite song. For instance, to the tune of "She'll Be Coming Round the Mountain" describe whatever you and your child are doing at the moment:

We'll be playing with my train set all day long,
We'll be playing with my train set all day long.
We'll be playing with my train set,
We'll be playing with my train set,
We'll be playing with my train set all day long.

I am dancing with my mommy to this song,
I am dancing with my mommy to this song.
I am dancing with my mommy,
I am dancing with my mommy,
I am dancing with my mommy to this song.

Mon	Tue	Wed	Thu	Fri	Sat
1	2	3	4	5	6
8	9	10	11	12	13
15	16	17	18	19	20
22	23	24	25	26	27
29	30	31			

167

count the days

Teach your child about time and scheduling by
hanging a month-view calendar at his eye level. Let
him mark special days—birthdays, family trips, and
play dates—with stickers or small drawings. For each
day, write in what you're going to do, or what you did.

168

take your crayons to go

Cut a rectangle of fabric from the seat of a discarded
pair of blue jeans, making sure the piece you choose
includes one of the back pockets. Then help your
child use nontoxic glue to attach the fabric to the
front cover of a spiral-bound sketchbook. When
the glue is dry, she can fill the pocket with crayons
and take her art journal on a drawing expedition.

4+

4 years & up

169

make a treasure box

Give your child a cigar box or shoe box, nontoxic
markers, stickers, ribbons, and other materials to
decorate a box for his treasures. He might even line
the box with fabric in a related pattern, such as a
baseball motif for a baseball card collection.

170

visit a music shop

It's never too soon for the musical bug to bite your child. Take her to a music shop to browse, listen to customers testing out new instruments, and maybe try out a floor model keyboard, drum, or triangle. Don't want to leave empty-handed? Consider buying a child-friendly instrument like a kazoo, a tambourine, or a harmonica.

171

be a sandbox archaeologist

Read or talk about archaeology, then outfit your child
with some tools of the trade: small shovels or spoons,
a strainer, a paintbrush, tweezers, and a magnifying
glass. Hide doll dishes, dollhouse furniture, and other
evidence of a fanciful civilization in a sandbox and
then turn him loose to discover them.

4+

4 years & up

172

pop up like a weasel

Chase your child around in a circle, and teach her to
"pop!" into the air like the weasel in this rhyme.

All around the cobbler's bench
The monkey chased the weasel.
The monkey thought 'twas all in fun,
Pop! goes the weasel.

173

make a telephone

Teach your child to make a cup-and-string telephone. Punch a hole in the bottoms of two paper cups and connect them with a long thin string (such as dental floss) knotted inside the cup. Take turns talking and listening. If you use the cups with the string stretched taut, your "telephone" really does amplify sound.

174

light up with lava

A staple of the '60s, lava lamps are back—and they fascinate preschoolers. A lava lamp makes a groovy light if you place it where it won't be knocked over. Check that it's listed for safety by the Underwriters Laboratories (UL), and make sure it doesn't get too hot.

175

construct with candy

You and your child don't need a fancy building set to be creative. Get out a box of toothpicks and a bag of gumdrops and see what the two of you can build together. A horse? An alien? A house?

176

expand your musical horizons

Your four-year-old is developing musical preferences at this stage, so it's a great time to expose him to different kinds of music. Invite him to listen and dance to classical, bluegrass, jazz, funk, and world music. Talk about the music afterward. What kind does he like listening to best? What's the most fun to dance to?

177

sculpt a,b,c...

Using colored clay, join your child in making different letters and numbers. It's a hands-on way to help her learn to recognize the ABCs and the 10 numerals, plus it's a great way to encourage creative sculpting.

178

visit the library

A trip to the library is always great fun. Let your child browse the shelves, choose a special book, and check out the artwork displayed in the children's section. In most libraries, a kid just has to be able to sign his name in order to be a card-carrying book lover, so now's the time for him to apply for his very first library card. How very grown-up!

179

provide privacy

As your preschooler grows and becomes more independent, she may sometimes want time alone. Make sure there's a quiet space in your house where your child can go to be on her own to unwind or just play. A corner outfitted with big pillows and a blanket works fine.

180

join the fan club

Fan-making is the perfect diversion on a hot day. Invite your child to decorate a piece of construction paper with nontoxic markers (he can go with abstract designs if he likes, or perhaps a frosty motif of penguins, polar bears, or snowflakes). Then show him how to fold the paper into pleats and chill out together.

181

plant a tree together

A tree is a wonderful thing for your child to grow
up with. Help her plant a sapling in your yard
(or, if you live in a city, in a relative's yard), and
visit the tree with her often to check on its growth.
A deciduous (leaf-bearing) tree also lets her watch
for seasonal changes. Taking her picture beside
the tree once a year is a great way to chronicle her
development, too. Someday she may even tell her own
children, "I remember when I planted this tree."

182

"he kicks...
He scores! Hey,
I'm getting way
better at soccer!"

4+

4 years & up

183

make party poppers

Help your child cut a piece of colored tissue paper
so it's wide enough to cover a cardboard toilet
paper tube widthwise and is 6 inches (15 cm) longer
than the tube. Ask him to center the tube on the paper
and roll it so it's covered, then tie a piece of yarn or
ribbon around one end to close and gather the paper.
Have him insert small, child-safe candies and toys
into the tube's open end, then tie up that end. Let
him loose with nontoxic glue, glitter, and stickers to
decorate the poppers. They're great for parties and
for celebrating special occasions. Tailor the poppers'
decorations and contents to the theme, be it dogs,
dinosaurs, pirates, princesses, or whatever else
captures your child's imagination.

184
rhyme with numbers

Preschoolers can act out this rhyme, or use it to keep the rhythm while jumping rope.

4+

4 years & up

One, two, buckle my shoe.
Three, four, knock at the door.
Five, six, pick up sticks.
Seven, eight, lay them straight.
Nine, ten, a big fat hen.
Eleven, twelve, dig and delve.
Thirteen, fourteen, maids a-courting.
Fifteen, sixteen, maids in the kitchen.
Seventeen, eighteen, maids in waiting.
Nineteen, twenty, my plate's empty.

185

transform seeds into art

Collect seeds in the spring or fall: maple wings, dandelion seeds, milkweed fluff, cottonwood puffs—whatever grows in your neck of the woods. Or just let your child pick out some seed packets at the store. Set her up with some sturdy paper, nontoxic paints, and child-safe glue, and watch her incorporate the seeds into a textured artwork. You might want to save some seeds to plant together, too.

186

recite poetry

Read your child some great poetry: works by Robert Louis Stevenson, Shel Silverstein, Douglas Florian, Jack Prelutsky, and many others are friendly, funny, and easy for four-year-olds to understand and enjoy.

187

befriend animals

If you don't have pets of your own, introduce your child to some dogs at the park, or visit with friends' cats. Teach him to approach animals safely and respectfully. Be his role model as he learns that the cat at the dry cleaner's can be grouchy, but the dog next door loves to be scratched behind her ears. Make sure he lets animals come to him and gets the owners' permission before he pets them or gives them treats.

4+

4 years & up

188

mix up pink lemonade

Feeling in the pink? Invite your child to flavor (and color) a pitcher of lemonade with ¼ cup (60 ml) of grenadine syrup. Once she's stirred it up, serve it in ice-filled glasses. Have her add a cherry to each one.

189

splash around

Engage your child in some watery fun. If he's learning to swim, head down to the pool and play games that make the most of those skills, like retrieving floating pool toys or racing you from one side of the pool to the other. Or just stay home: the bathtub's a great "laboratory" for experiments aimed at discovering which kinds of objects float and which ones sink. (Remember to always supervise water play.)

190

festoon a room

Help your child fold squares of colorful tissue paper into fans, in quarters or eighths, and show her how to cut shapes out of the edges, much as you'd cut out paper snowflakes. Unfold the paper and together hang the designs on a line of string.

191

go green together

Talk to your child about the environment and how we can help protect it. Then enlist him to make your home more "green." Together turn off lights, turn down the thermostat, put on sweaters, and don't run the water while brushing your teeth. Soon your young environmentalist will do these things on his own.

192

make a special paper doll

Cut out your child's head and face from a printed digital photo or snapshot (the bigger the better). Draw a simple body shape on stiff posterboard, then help her glue on the photo cutout to make a paper doll. Using lighter paper, trace around the body shape to make simple clothing shapes she can cut out and color as she wishes. Use a reusable-glue stick (similar to the not-too-sticky adhesive used in sticky notes) from a crafts or office supply store to make the clothes easy to put on and take off. Got a group shot of your child with her playmates or siblings? Your child can make some familiar friends for her doll.

193

"marbles are cool... I love to count them, sort them, or just watch them as they roll around.**"**

4+

4 years & up

194

stencil a shirt

Have your child cut a geometric or animal shape out of heavy paper. Use masking tape on the bottom of the shape to attach it to the front of a light-colored T-shirt. While wearing old clothes, your child can dip a large paintbrush into fabric paint and rub his finger along the bristles to spray paint around the shape. When he's done, remove the stencil, let the shirt dry, then set the image by putting the shirt in a dryer on low heat.

195

prompt with pictures

Photo reminders—say, of your child feeding the dog or brushing her teeth—are a fun way to prompt her to do her daily tasks. Together select and mount the pictures on posterboard to hang in her room.

196

make tiny footprints

Teach your child how to make fairy footprints at the
beach by making a fist and pressing the pinkie side
into the sand. Then use your thumb and fingertips to
add imprints for the toes. Make prints for right and
left feet, or even make prints "walking" on the beach.

4+

4 years & up

197

design signature specs

To increase the chances that your child
will actually wear his sunglasses, let him personalize
them with small stickers, or use child-safe glue to
attach charms or beads. Choose children's sunglasses
that are labeled "100 percent UV Protection."

198

have a heart

Show your preschooler how to make hearts by cutting a teardrop shape along the edge of a folded piece of paper. Get her started by drawing the cutting line for her; before long she'll be turning out dozens of hearts for cards and crafts projects all by herself.

199

encourage charity

4+

4 years & up

Take your child shopping so he can pick out a toy to donate to a holiday charity drive. Now and again, ask him if he has any dolls, games, or plush animals he'd like to give to a less-fortunate child. Shelters, charity stores, and hospitals often welcome gently used toys.

200

get your mouth around this

This Mother Goose tongue twister is a kids' classic.

Peter Piper picked a peck of pickled peppers;
A peck of pickled peppers Peter Piper picked.
If Peter Piper picked a peck of pickled peppers,
Where's the peck of pickled peppers Peter Piper picked?

201

make your own crafts show

Set aside a special day when your child invites a
few friends over to make crafty items like necklaces,
picture frames, paintings—whatever captures each
young artist's imagination. Then set up a table or two
outside and display their handiwork. Who knows,
they might even make some sales to your neighbors!

202

share tee time

A four-year-old can learn to swing a child's lightweight bat at a softball. To improve her odds of actually hitting it, use a tee designed to hold the ball at the right height. Be your little slugger's cheerleader and outfielder as she hones her skill.

203

go primitive

Share some storybooks about prehistoric times, then turn a grocery bag into an animal hide or a cave wall. Have your child scrunch the bag up, then flatten it out again until it's soft and wrinkled. Then outfit him with colored chalks for drawing stick figures of people and animals on the intriguingly primitive surface.

204
grill s'mores

Supervise your child as she toasts a marshmallow over the grill (a long barbecue fork will keep her a safe distance from the flames or coals). Help her sandwich it with a square of milk chocolate between two graham crackers. Rainy day? Assemble some s'mores and pop them in the microwave for a few seconds.

205
design jewelry

A four-year-old's fine motor skills and emerging design sense enable him to make some pretty snazzy necklaces, bracelets, and rings. If he enjoys crafting jewelry, visit a bead shop and pick up a few special beads or look for a book on simple beading projects.

206

make a moose

Teach your child how to make a moose by tracing her foot (with her shoe on) and her hands (with her fingers spread to make "antlers") on brown paper. Then have her cut out the shapes and glue them onto white paper. She can give her moose personality by coloring in a big black nose and some goofy eyes.

207

read together

Your child observes and learns by watching what you do, so show him that you love to read! Have regular family reading times together. When you read to your child, pause occasionally and ask him what he thinks will happen next. He can also provide sound effects.

208

"see my garden grow...
Planting seedlings is
easier than waiting
for those poky
seeds to sprout!"

209

create a creature

Join your preschooler in cutting out animal body parts and faces from magazines, then give her paper and glue so she can arrange the pieces to fashion funny and fanciful new hybrid animals.

4+

4 years & up

210

fascinate with fingerprints

Teach your child to be a fingerprint expert. Have him press a fingertip against clear glass, then sprinkle the spot he touched with baby powder, blow or brush off the excess, and pick up the resulting image by laying clear tape over it and pulling it up gently. Give him a magnifying glass so he can compare the whorls on the tape with his real finger. A perfect match!

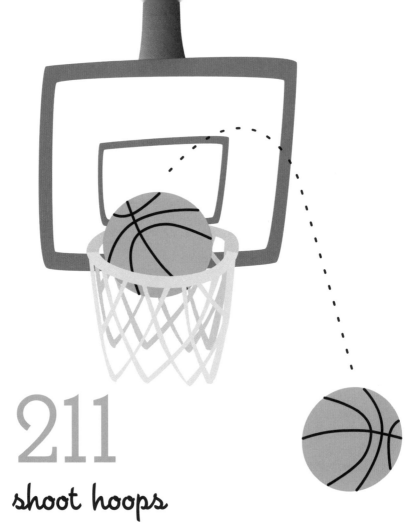

211

shoot hoops

Playing basketball lets your child practice all kinds of gross motor skills: running, dribbling a ball, passing a ball, and—most fun of all—shooting baskets. To nurture your future all-star, put up a kid-sized basketball hoop, or find one at a park or school playground.

212

phone home

Teach your child your home phone number, and let him practice calling it from your house (he'll get your voice mail or a busy signal) and from other phones, including cell phones. This is also a good time to remind him to call 911 in an emergency.

213

enjoy a game of checkers

Four is a great age to learn checkers, a wonderful game for people of different generations to play together. Play at home or pack a portable set. Checkers is an amusing way to pass the time—say, while you're waiting for a meal in a restaurant.

214

spot fish

Four-year-olds love learning about nature. At a pond
or a creek, teach her to spot ripples appearing on
the water's surface as fish rise to eat insects. Putting
on polarized sunglasses will give you both a better
chance of glimpsing the fish through the water.

215

have a drinking-straw race

4+

4 years & up

Draw an obstacle course in chalk on a sidewalk, then show your child how to race a small piece of crumpled paper or foil through the course by blowing on it through a drinking straw. He can compete with you or a friend to be the first to blow across the finish line.

216

show your dog who's boss

If you have a dog, it's important to make sure he minds your child the same way he does older family members. A fun training activity is for you and your child to go to different rooms, each with a few special dog treats. Take turns calling, "Jake! Come!" and reward your pet with treats when he responds. As a bonus, your dog gets a good workout while he learns.

217

hang out at the firehouse

Call ahead to arrange a visit for your child (and maybe some of her friends) to check out your local fire station. Depending on what's going on when you arrive, she may be able to see the fire trucks close up, watch them being washed and serviced, or talk with firefighters. Some stations offer small gifts like coloring books or plastic firefighter's helmets to kids who visit.

218

climb higher

Seek out playgrounds with climbing equipment such as monkey bars, a climbing net, a firefighter's pole, or even a low rock-climbing wall. Supervise your child as he goes up and down—and improves his gross motor skills along the way.

219

love the lovie

Even as your child ventures out into the world more independently, she might still appreciate the chance to reassure herself with a special cuddly toy she associates with home and family. Let her take her lovie with her whenever she wants, since it helps her feel safe while she's pushing her boundaries.

220

exit gracefully

Help your preschooler make a smooth transition when it's time to end a fun event like a play date. Give him some warning ("We'll have to go home in 15 minutes") and a couple of notices ("Let's find your shoes now, because it's almost time to go"), and encourage him as he learns to leave quickly and without any fuss.

221

keep an animal log

Read about local animal species together, then take a walk or watch from a window to spot some real-life specimens. Start a list of all the furry friends your little naturalist discovers and ask her to draw a picture of each one next to its name.

222

pour milk

Encourage your child's growing sense of autonomy and accomplishment by letting him pour milk from a small pitcher (which is easier to handle than a carton) into his glass or his cereal bowl on his own.

223

swap books

Invite a small group of parents and kids to join you and your child in a book swap. Ask each attendee to bring several good used books to trade (don't ask your child to part with special favorites—and you can hold on to yours, too). Leave some books and take some, and share a snack and maybe a story or two. Everyone goes home with new reading material—for free!

224

fill in the speech balloons

Look for pictures of people in old newspapers or magazines and help your child glue cartoon speech balloons into the scene. Talk about what the people are doing, then have your child dictate the dialogue.

225

count with number towers

Help your child cut five "towers" from colored paper and have her write the numbers 1 through 10 from the bottom to the top of the first tower. On the next, start at the bottom and count together as she writes 11 through 20. Keep going, with each tower containing the next 10 numbers. Arrange the towers side by side to help your child count by tens. Hang them on her wall, and soon she'll have no trouble counting.

226

"tying shoes is tricky...
But with your help and
patience, I'll get it soon.**"**

227

be prepared

Playing "What if..." is a good way to teach your child
how to handle emergencies. "What if you smell smoke
or see a fire?" (Tell an adult or call 911 immediately.)
"What if a ball rolls into the street?" (Ask an adult to
get it.) "What if the kitty scratches you?" (Ask an adult
for some first-aid help—and a hug to make it all better.)

228

protect your veggie patch

Save scratched CDs or any that come in your junk
mail, then help your child affix twine to hang them
from branches or stakes in your vegetable garden.
As the CDs spin and twinkle in the sunlight, they'll
keep birds from eating the fruits of your labors.

229

write with light

Have your child lie on his back in a darkened room
(with you there for company, of course) and use
a small flashlight to "write" letters or draw simple
pictures on the ceiling. See if you can guess what
he's writing. Take turns writing and guessing.

230

add it up

Learning math doesn't have to involve paper,
blackboards, or calculators. Lay the foundation for
learning about fractions by pointing out the difference
between a half and a whole cup, the way the pizza is
divided into eight slices, or that sharing four cookies
with a friend means that they each get two.

231

be inspired by books

Read some books together by renowned kids' author Eric Carle (*The Very Hungry Caterpillar* and *The Very Busy Spider* are some of his popular titles) and try out his style of collage. Finger paint different patterns on white or colored paper, then cut and paste the patterns into collages of animal and nature shapes.

232

bottle the ocean

Fill a clear plastic bottle halfway with blue-tinted water, add a toy boat or plastic fish, then fill almost to the top with mineral oil. Apply hot glue to the neck of the bottle with a glue gun (adults only), screw on the lid, and let the glue set. Lay the bottle on its side, then invite your child to rock it gently to make "waves."

233

catch and release

4+

4 years & up

If you're lucky enough to live in an area that has fireflies during the summer, help your child catch some during a balmy evening. Besides giving off an enchanting glow, fireflies fly slowly and don't bite, so they're ideal subjects for informal nature study. House them temporarily in a glass jar (punch tiny holes in the lid to let in air). Let your child study the living lanterns for an hour or so, then let them go so they can get on with their buggy adventures.

234

bake monkey bread

If you make or buy the bread dough for a basic white loaf and melt the butter, your child can do all the other steps except putting it into the oven and taking it out again. Have your child break off pieces of dough, roll them into walnut-sized balls, and dip them into a bowl containing cooled melted butter. Next, have him drop the buttery balls of dough into a Bundt pan, layering them until the pan is two-thirds full. Bake as directed by the recipe or the package instructions. Once the bread has cooled, remove it from the pan and invite him to dive in and just pull the balls apart with his hands—the way a monkey would. For a yummy sweet variation, have your child roll each dough ball in cinnamon and sugar before placing it in the pan.

235

make multilingual wishes

Teach your child to say "happy birthday" to family and friends in a few different languages.

Arabic: eid milaad saeed
(aid meela-ad sa-yeed)
French: bon anniversaire
(bun ahn-nee-vair-sair)
Japanese: otanjou-bi omedetou gozaimasu
(oh-tahn-joh-bee oh-meh-deh-toh goh-zah-ee-mahs)
Spanish: feliz cumpleaños
(fay-leez coom-play-ahn-yohs)

236

set up a workspace

Dedicate a space where your child can draw, write, and dream. Having a special spot devoted to those pursuits reinforces their importance, while giving her a sense of ownership, independence, and maturity. Encourage her to personalize her workspace, for example, by decorating plastic cups with colored paper or tape to make holders for crayons or pencils.

237

make a piggy bank

Cut a slit in the plastic top of a tall, cylindrical potato chip can. Help your child cover the sides of the can with wrapping or construction paper. Hold the paper in place for him while he tapes it around the can (or switch roles, if that's easier for him). Now that he's got his homemade piggy bank, talk to him about how money works (toys don't grow on trees!) and encourage him to start saving some of his own. He might even earn some coins by doing extra chores around the house or in the yard.

238

"tuck in those corners...
I love making my bed
all by myself in the
morning. See? No
wrinkles!"

239

string paper clips

Give your child a box of paper clips to make into chains and necklaces. With colored paper clips, she can experiment with making patterns as well.

240

host a backyard olympics

Gather some of your child's friends together and set up a circuit of active games for them. You might want to include an obstacle course of hula hoops laid flat on the grass to hop through, a garden hose stretched out as a "beam" to walk across, beanbags and wet sponges to toss, or other kid-pleasing activities. Start a child or two off on each activity. When you blow a whistle, have each child move on to the next activity.

241

exercise creative license

Challenge your child to make a silly phrase using the letters on the license plate of the car in front of yours. For instance, if the license plate has "TLB" on it, he might come up with "turtles love ballet."

242

make a rockin' paperweight

Have your child cut out a photo she likes from a magazine and affix it to a smooth stone with nontoxic glue. To keep the picture from yellowing, thin some more glue with a little water and have her paint it over the picture with a small paintbrush. When the glue's dry, she'll have her own personal desk accessory.

243

race ducks

In a large wading pool, line your child and his friends up and give each one a rubber duck. At your signal, each kid tries to urge his or her duck to the other side without touching it, just by splashing the water around it. The first child to splash a duck to the other side is the winner. (Remember to always supervise water play.)

4+

4 years & up

5+
from five years & up

At age five, literacy takes a leap, coordination improves, and concentration increases—in fact, your child is more adept at just about everything. His social circle expands to include new friends and classmates. He's also likely to have closer relationships with siblings, grandparents, and cousins. His world is growing larger in other senses, too, as shown by his increased concern for animals and the environment. But even with his ever-expanding horizons, in your child's book, you're still number one.

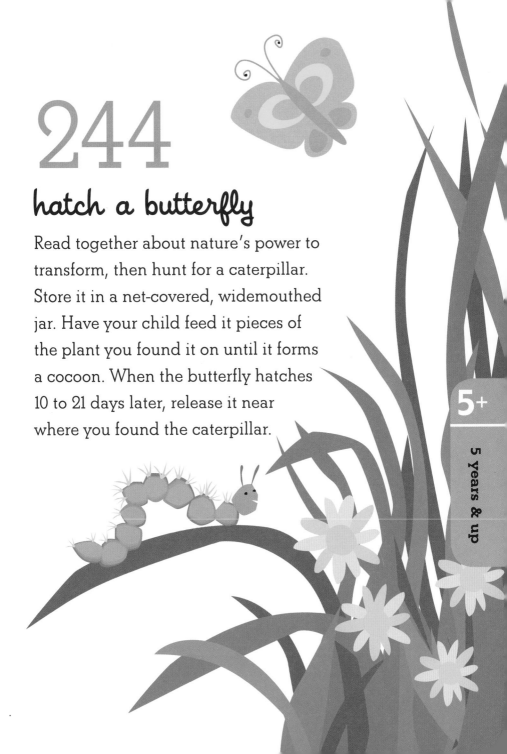

244

hatch a butterfly

Read together about nature's power to
transform, then hunt for a caterpillar.
Store it in a net-covered, widemouthed
jar. Have your child feed it pieces of
the plant you found it on until it forms
a cocoon. When the butterfly hatches
10 to 21 days later, release it near
where you found the caterpillar.

5+

5 years & up

245

picture the alphabet

Look through old magazines together for photos that
illustrate letters of the alphabet: an ape for A, a ball for
B, and so on. For do-it-yourself flash cards, have your
child cut the photos out, paste them on cardboard
with nontoxic glue, and write the letter on the back.

246

make a book

Use a three-hole punch to make holes in a dozen or
so sheets of white drawing paper and put them in a
binder. For a cover, ask your child to draw a picture on
a sheet of paper and help her glue it to the front of the
binder with child-safe glue. She can draw, doodle, and
write in her new book. You can jump-start literacy by
having her dictate words for you to write on the pages.

247

play "slap jack"

This game promotes turn-taking and pattern recognition, and it's easy for little hands since all your cards don't have to be held at once. Deal out a standard deck of 52 cards evenly between you and your child, but don't look at them yet. Taking turns, pick up a card from your stack and lay it face up on the table to create a third stack. If the card is a jack, the goal is to try to place your hand on top of it before your opponent does, winning you the jack and all the cards under it. The winner is the player who ends up with all of the cards.

248

find time for a rhyme

Kids love rhythm and silly words, especially
when they tell a story. Dig through your
(or the library's) bookshelves and find some
classic lines of poetry to read and enjoy
together. Great poems for children this age
include Edward Lear's "The Owl and the
Pussycat" and Lewis Carroll's masterpiece
of nonsense, "Jabberwocky."

249

create collages

Collage basics are a sturdy piece of paper or cardboard for a foundation, scissors, plenty of nontoxic glue, and of course, imagination. Beyond that, collages can be made of just about anything: scraps of wrapping paper, ribbons, buttons, stickers, pictures cut from magazines, and paint samples. Or invite your child to make a tribute to nature by using materials like bark, seeds, leaves, grasses, and pressed flowers. If he needs a jump start, suggest a collage of pictures of foods he enjoys, a seasonal motif such as spring flowers or autumn leaves, or just a mix of assorted items in his favorite colors.

5+

5 years & up

250
learn to jump rope

Have your child start with the rope on the ground behind her. Then have her swing it over her head to the ground in front of her, then jump over it as it lies there. Practice (and a few demonstrations) will soon have her jumping on her own.

251
craft a felt necklace

Teach your child how to make a necklace by first cutting felt into small squares, triangles, or any other shape he fancies. Then help him use a child-safe crafts needle and sturdy thread to string the shapes together into a necklace.

252

make shoe-venirs

Got an old pair of your child's sneakers and a
permanent marker? Your child can use them to gather
her friends' signatures, marking a special event.

253

try on a new identity

A regular paper plate (not the heavy-duty kind) is the
ideal size and weight for making a kid's mask. Punch
out two holes, one on each side of the plate. Thread
elastic through them, knot the ends, and let your child
try the mask on so you can mark the eyeholes. Have
him remove the mask and cut out the holes. Let him
loose with art supplies and his imagination to become
whatever he fancies: wolf, space alien, or clown.

254

" glass, paper, plastic...
Sorting the recycling
is easy, and I feel good
about helping the planet. "

255

make a comb kazoo

Give your child a clean, fine-tooth pocket comb
and a piece of thin, strong paper. (Wax paper works
well, but you can experiment with other types.) Have
her wrap the comb's teeth in the paper, then press
her lips gently against the paper and hum strongly
to make a hair-raising tune.

256

write the book on safety

Have a family safety drill covering topics such as
where to meet in case everyone has to leave the
house quickly. Ask your child to take snapshots of
key parts of the route with a disposable camera
and paste the photos on paper. Then have him
dictate the captions for his home safety manual.

5+

5 years & up

257

go nutty

Ask your child to assist you as you measure and pour
2 cups (475 ml) of salted, roasted almonds or cashews
into a blender or food processor. Blend until smooth.
Let her use a butter knife to spread the nut butter on
crackers or bread—enough for both of you!

258

weave a pot holder

You probably did this craft as a kid yourself. Buy a child's weaving kit with a small square loom and cotton loops. Sit down with your child and teach him how to weave a pot holder. The tradition continues!

259

make an instant finger puppet

Show your child how to transform her hand into a finger puppet by planting the tips of her thumb, pointer, ring, and pinkie fingers on the table to make the legs of a "creature," using her middle finger to form its head and long neck. Draw a simple face on the tip of her middle finger with a washable nontoxic marker, and see if she can walk the creature across the table. Sound effects like growls or barks are a plus.

260

ride a two-wheeler

Depending on your child's height and dexterity, he
may be ready to graduate from a tricyle to a bicycle.
Straddling the bike, he should be able to put his feet
flat on the ground; seated, the balls of his feet should
touch the ground. For most five-year-olds, that means
selecting a bike with 12- to 14-inch (30- to 36-cm)
wheels. Start with training wheels touching the
ground and move them up a little bit every week. Give
him lots of encouragement as he gradually improves
with each ride. Buy a helmet along with the bike, and
make sure your child uses it every time he rides.

261

go beyond books

Your library offers great kids' attractions besides books. Check out movies, audiobooks, and computer games, or ask for a schedule of activities so you and your child can attend free movie showings, author events, storytimes, and other special events.

262

sew a shirt pillow

Sew closed the sleeve and bottom hem openings of a beloved but outgrown shirt. Invite your child to stuff it with handfuls of fiberfill from the crafts store. Once she's got it nice and plump, sew up the neck opening to make a comfy pillow she can lounge around on.

263

do a good deed

Five-year-olds love helping and pleasing others. Put those altruistic instincts to good use by encouraging your child to do something nice for someone else—bring the neighbors' newspaper up to their door, check a pet's water dish on a hot day, share a treat with a friend or younger sibling. It's fine to praise him gently for helping others (sometimes a smile or a wink is enough), but ultimately you want him to help just because it's the right thing to do. "May I help?" should become as natural to your child as saying "Please" and "Thank you."

264

make silhouettes

Tape a piece of white paper to a wall, darken the room, and ask your child to sit about 2 feet (60 cm) in front of the paper. Shine a bright light, such as a desk lamp, at the side of her face (have her close her eyes if the light bothers her). Outline her shadow on the white paper, then have her cut out the outline, place it on a piece of black construction paper, and trace around it in chalk. Next she can cut out the black silhouette and glue it to a white piece of paper. Then let her seat you or a stuffed animal with a distinctive profile on the chair and trace and cut out that silhouette.

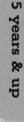

5+

5 years & up

265

paint like a master

Look together at pictures of Michelangelo's Sistine Chapel. Explain that the artist painted the higher sections while lying on his back on a tall scaffolding. Then let your child try it—closer to the ground, of course. Place a drop cloth beneath a low table, tape art paper to the table's underside, and ask him to put on a smock or an old T-shirt in case of messy drips. (It may be a good idea to have him wear some goggles as well, to avoid any paint splashing in his eyes.) Then equip him with a paintbrush dipped in washable nontoxic paint and invite him to recline beneath the table and paint a favorite storybook scene. There's nothing like a new perspective to inspire great art!

266

design snowflakes

Teach your child to fold circles or squares of thin paper and cut slashes and shapes into both the open and the folded sides to make snowy designs. For a shimmering effect, have her dab the snowflakes with a glue stick and sprinkle them with silver glitter.

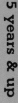

267

celebrate japanese-style

Research Japanese festivals at the library or online
and celebrate the ones that appeal to your child.
For instance, on Children's Day in Japan, families
fly streamers in the shape of fish. Another Japanese
celebration with potential kid appeal is the Bean
Throwing Festival, when people toss a few beans for
good luck, and eat one bean for each year of their age.

268

write in shaving cream

Put lots of shaving cream on a baking sheet, then invite your child to smooth it out and draw a letter or a number in it. Guess what he's made: "Is it the letter *S*? The number *5*?" He'll love teaching you for a change! (Keep shaving cream away from his mouth and eyes.)

269

ask a riddle

Your youngster's growing vocabulary and verbal skills make hearing and making up riddles a favorite form of humor. Try out this giggle-inducing one:

What's brown and dangerous?
Shark-infested pudding!

5+

5 years & up

270

study bugs

Get some books from the library or do online research to learn about insects together. The more your child knows about creepy crawlies, the less creepy they are.

271

use a magnetic bulletin board

A magnetic bulletin board can help your child get organized—and express herself. Hang the board at kid height in her room or another spot she frequents, then demonstrate how to put drawings, party invitations, or photos onto the board with an array of interesting magnets. It will not only remind her of events she's looking forward to, it can also be a way to store mementos of relatives, friends, and vacations.

272

share sweet sushi

Make sweet "sushi" together. Instead of sticky rice, use treats made from puffed-rice cereal and marshmallow. Tuck gummy fish in the center to take the place of the real thing, and wrap green or blue fruit rolls to stand in for seaweed. Try eating the treats with chopsticks. Your child might be intrigued enough to want to sample real sushi.

273

remember vital info

At five, your child should know his address and phone number as well as his parents' full names. Repetition helps kids learn. Make up a song with the information, or put it to the tune of a favorite song. Sing it over and over until he knows it by heart. Revisit it now and again to make sure he remembers these vital basics.

274

appreciate music

Most communities have free musical events—ranging from symphony rehearsals to outdoor fairs—open to the public. Go together as a family, taking advantage of any opportunities to speak with musicians afterward or to take a look at the instruments up close.

275

5+

5 years & up

"round and round
and round—oops...
It's tricky at first, but
playing with a hula
hoop is lots of fun."

276

play red light, green light

Your child will get a kick out of this old classic.
The player who is "it" stands at one end of the
yard, while the other children line up at the other.
The child who's "it" stands with his back turned
to the line of kids and calls out "Green light!"
The other kids run toward her, but must stop
when he yells "Red light!" and turns around.
Any children she catches still running must go back
to the starting line. "It" then turns back around
and repeats the red light–green light cycle until
one child reaches and tags her. That child
is now "it," and the game starts over again.

277

leaf through a scrapbook

Take a stroll outside with your child and invite him to pick up leaves that appeal to him. He can press them into a scrapbook at home, and together you can use a guide to identify the trees they came from. To help him learn about seasonal change, go on another excursion to collect leaves during a different time of year.

278

pop some corn

Popcorn has it all: sound effects, enticing aroma, yummy taste, and near-instant gratification. Make some in the microwave and listen to the pops together. If you have a popper, show your child how to put the kernels in, put on the lid, press "start," and stand back!

279

visit a planetarium

Stargazing with your child on a clear, warm night is one of life's great pleasures. But sometimes it's better to head indoors to a place where you can see the stars and planets in comfort and with greater predictability. Take a trip together to the nearest planetarium and enjoy the sky show.

280

design a notepad

Ask your child to make some small line drawings and select her favorite. Then take it to a copy shop to get it reproduced on notepads. Personalized notepads make wonderful presents for teachers, friends, and relatives.

281

read all about it

Take dictation from your child to produce a few short
news stories about your family's exploits using a
simple computer publishing program (or just your best
handwriting on a piece of paper). Add a masthead
and headlines, then ask him to make some illustrations
(or help you pick out a few photos) to accompany the
articles he composed for your family gazette.

282

get slimy

Whip up some slime with your child! Help her
measure a one-to-one ratio of water and corn starch.
Have her mix them (adding a splash of her favorite
food coloring) until it's smooth—and plenty slimy.

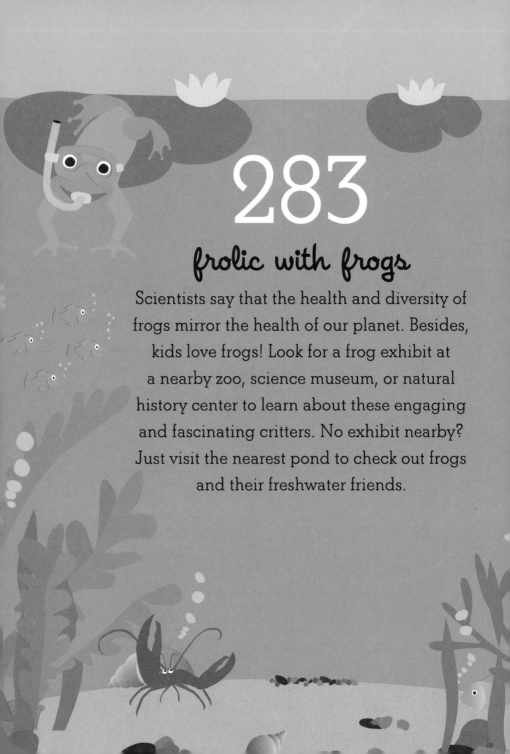

283

frolic with frogs

Scientists say that the health and diversity of frogs mirror the health of our planet. Besides, kids love frogs! Look for a frog exhibit at a nearby zoo, science museum, or natural history center to learn about these engaging and fascinating critters. No exhibit nearby? Just visit the nearest pond to check out frogs and their freshwater friends.

284

act it out

A full-fledged game of charades is still a bit challenging for your five-year-old, but she'll relish the chance to play a scaled-down version. Take turns acting out the tasks that go on in her everyday world—such as combing hair, brushing teeth, or driving a car—and then try to guess what the other person is doing. Move on to imitate an animal for each other to identify: leap like a frog, gallop like a horse, or "swim" like a fish. If she's loving it, take the game a step further and act like her favorite storybook characters. Can she tell that you're skipping down a path with a basket for Grandma, like Little Red Riding Hood? Can you spot her monkeying around like Curious George?

5+

5 years & up

285

a-maze a cat

Join your child in an art project that's fun for the two of you—and for the family cat. Cut the bottoms out of several brown paper grocery bags and tape them together end to end to make a maze for your cat (try to make at least one "tunnel" branching off from the main one). Roll in a small ball to entice your cat to explore.

286

take a deeper look

Unleash your child's inner scientist by helping him glimpse the magical structures of simple crystals. Set him up in your kitchen "laboratory" with a microscope and staples like table salt, sea salt, or white sugar. Then let him discover how those tiny specks look up close.

287

kick up a sporty storm

Head outside with your child to get a kick out of playing with balls. Warm up by kicking a soccer ball (or a big rubber ball) back and forth while standing still, then practice passing while running. Once he's a ground-ball pro, show him how to shoot "goals," taking aim at the space between two trees or two park benches. Or keep it light: see who can kick the ball the farthest, the highest, or in the silliest way.

288

relocate storytime

On a warm spring or summer evening, surprise your child by moving your nightly storytime outdoors and reading together by flashlight.

289

"cereal, milk, tea, bananas... Playing pretend grocery store is almost as much fun as going to the real store."

290

play with numbers

Without making it feel like a lesson, engage your child in tasks that involve numerical logic. For instance, show him how to use a measuring tape and he'll likely measure everything in sight. Ask him to help you weigh the cat: have him hold the cat while you weigh them both, then weigh just your child and show him how you subtract that number from the first one to get kitty's weight.

291

draw on your patience

Drawing together is always a pleasure. You can help your child learn about teamwork if you share one nontoxic marker and each wait your turn.

292

watch the weather

Teach your child weather-forecasting folklore, like how rain's on the way when the wind blows the leaves so their undersides show. Or how a ring of light around the moon means a cold snap is coming. Watch for these portents together, and keep a weather chart to see if they really do predict the weather accurately.

293

go digital

If you're techno-savvy and into the latest gadgets, your child can be, too. Many libraries let patrons check out electronic books online; if yours is one of them, check out some books your child can listen to on a computer or a portable MP3 player. (Protect her hearing by making sure the volume's not too high.)

294

get a jump on juggling

Juggling starts with one simple move: tossing an object from one hand to the other in a circular motion. Help your future juggler catch on to the fun by providing him with different items to throw into the air, one at a time, grabbing each item as it falls down. Start with a scarf, which is easy to toss with one hand and catch with the other. Move on to a small beanbag, then to a soft foam ball. Once your child can throw and catch these items from hand to hand, make it more challenging. Can he do it while slowly walking forward? How about while he's standing on one foot?

5+

5 years & up

295

label treasures

Buy some polymer clay at a crafts store. Help your child shape some into a small disc, poke a hole in the top with a drinking straw, and press in raw alphabet noodles to spell out the name of a beloved plush animal. Remove the noodles and bake according to the directions on the clay. Make tags for all her favorite friends, and attach them with cord or ribbon.

296

jump through hoops

Gather a number of inexpensive hula hoops and lay them on the grass in different patterns—say, in pairs, or close together in a long line. Challenge your child to run, hop, or duckwalk along the course and back.

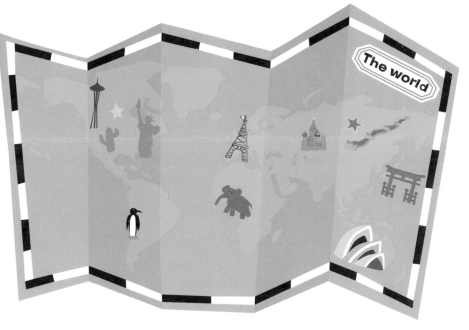

The world

297

map your child's world

Hang a world map on the wall of your child's room.
Use colored pins to mark different locations: red for
where family members live, green for the countries
your relatives came from, blue for places he's heard
about or seen in movies or on television. The concept
of the map may seem abstract at first, but eventually
it will start to make sense: "Hey—Grandpa's from
the country we read about in school today!"

5+

5 years & up

298

sing a song of spaghetti

Make a simple spaghetti dinner together and sing this
parody to the tune of "On Top of Old Smokey."

On top of spaghetti, all covered with cheese,
I lost my poor meatball when somebody sneezed.

It rolled off the table, and onto the floor,
And then my poor meatball rolled on out the door.

It rolled in the garden, and under a bush,
And then my poor meatball was nothing but mush.

If you eat spaghetti, all covered with cheese,
Hold onto your meatball—and don't ever sneeze!

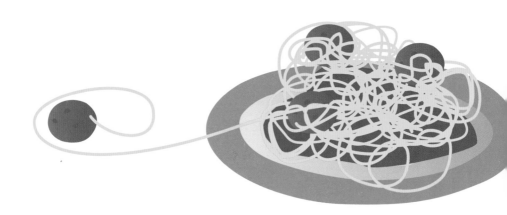

299

create an edible ocean

Have some seafaring fun with your youngster right in your kitchen. Mix up a bowl of blue gelatin, and put it in the refrigerator to set. Just before it's fully set, insert gummy fish candies in contrasting colors. Float a life preserver–shaped candy on top. Ahoy, matey!

300

decorate a pumpkin

Although carving a jack-o-lantern is an adult job, your child can decorate a pumpkin with simple materials. Help her use nontoxic glue to attach leaves for hair, a carrot tip for a witchy nose, marshmallows for eyes, or rows of corn for a gap-toothed smile. Then have her add finishing touches with nontoxic markers. Spooky!

5+

5 years & up

301

make a doll at home

Cut the top flaps, the bottom, and one side from
a small corrugated cardboard box, leaving three
sides to make an open house for small dolls or plush
animals. Use an art knife (adults only) to cut windows
and doors, then let your child go to town decorating
his toys' new abode with markers or crayons.

302

share your childhood secrets

Kids love hearing stories from your childhood
(especially about times you misbehaved or got into
trouble). So share some of your memories—and don't
be surprised if your child asks, "Tell me again about
the time you and Aunt Susan broke the clock."

303

whip up breakfast

Invite your five-year-old to flex her cooking muscles by making breakfast (with lots of adult supervision, of course). To make French toast, she can mix up eggs, milk, and a little vanilla in a bowl, then dip in bread slices. For a heartier dish, have her help you fry up eggs and sausages, teaching her how to break the eggs into a frying pan and use a fork to take the sausages out of the pan when they're done. Or she could keep things simple by popping bread into the toaster and topping the toast with butter and jam.

5+

5 years & up

304

shoot some laundry

Laundry day can be a slam dunk if you hang a laundry bag from a kid's basketball hoop mounted on the wall in your child's room. He'll love getting some throwing practice while keeping his room tidy.

305

rub different textures

Teach your little one to make rubbings by laying thin paper over three-dimensional surfaces and rubbing them with a peeled crayon or an art pastel. Start with coins or keys, and soon she'll see intriguing rubbing possibilities everywhere: a stone wall, tree bark, a bamboo mat. Make it a game by having her do a few rubbings; then you guess where they came from.

306

"tiger roars are fun...
But I also like being a
lion, or a puppy, or just
the rainbow kid. Let's
wipe the face paint off
and start all over again."

307

serve up a slush

Help your child make some slurpy slush—and learn
about salty science. Fill a large zip-top bag halfway
with ice and a cup of salt, then fill a smaller bag with
juice. Put the small bag, zipped, into the big one, and
zip it shut. Wait about 15 minutes for the salt and ice
solution to make the juice freeze, shaking it often.
Then hand him the little bag and a spoon—yum!

308

give thanks

Talk about gratitude together, and then encourage
your child to write a thank-you note. Help her with the
writing, if it's difficult—or encourage her to draw a
picture that expresses her appreciation for a kind act.

309

write a limerick

A limerick is a lighthearted five-line poem. The first, second, and fifth lines rhyme, as do the third and fourth. Kids love limericks, like this favorite:

A flea and a fly in a flue
Were caught, so what could they do?
Said the fly, "Let us flee."
"Let us fly," said the flea.
So they flew through a flaw in the flue.

Read some limericks together (Edward Lear's are classic), then see if you and your child can make up a few of your own. Get him started by feeding him a good first line ("There once was a lion who cried") and let him take it from there.

310

stitch a mail pouch

Fold a thin sheet of craft foam in half, punch holes along the sides, and help your child use ribbon to stitch it into a pouch. Hang it up so you have a mail pouch for leaving each other notes or special treats.

311

get to know a grasshopper

Teach your child how to catch a grasshopper (gently). Study the bug quickly before he hops away, or keep him in your bug house (see activity #1) for a little while. Give him some grass to eat. Look at his tiny face and see if you can spot the little holes along his side that he breathes through. What an amazing creature!

312

fold up art

Look at a book together on origami for kids, then help your child try her hand at making some simple forms. Buy squares of colored origami paper at the crafts store or give her squares cut from gift wrap, printed paper bags, or even plain printer or notebook paper.

313

create a puzzle

Lay eight wooden Popsicle sticks side by side with no gaps, and have your child use nontoxic glue to carefully attach a picture to the sticks. When the glue dries, separate the sticks using an art knife (adult job). Mix them up and let him reassemble the puzzle.

314

pen a comic strip

Draw or print a series of large boxes on plain paper
and show your child how to make her own comic
strips. She can start by using the boxes you made and
adding some simple characters like thumbprint people
or stick figures to tell a joke. Soon she'll be coming up
with her own funny or dramatic story lines.

315

make your own lotto

Help your child photograph landmarks in your town (such as statues, the fire station, and the middle school where he'll go in a few years). Glue the photos to a piece of white cardboard to make a lotto board, and laminate it so it's reusable. Ask him to put a check mark next to the picture of the landmarks he spots when you're driving or walking through town.

316

see fish fly

Help your child cut out several identical fish shapes, then color and decorate them. Staple two of them together, leaving one side open until she's stuffed it with crumpled newspaper. Make lots of them, and then hang a school of fish from the ceiling.

317

get the point

Look together at pointillist paintings: those in which the
images are made up of tiny dots. (Georges-Pierre Seurat
is one of the most famous pointillists.) Once you've
studied the style, help your child use nontoxic markers
to make a picture using the same technique.

318

experiment with invisibility

Give your child a cotton swab, some lemon juice,
and a white piece of paper, and invite him to dip the
swab in the juice to write a secret message or draw
a special picture for you. When it's dry, show
him how you can reveal the secret by running
a warm iron over the paper (adults only).

319

make "ice cream" cakes

Stand flat-bottomed ice cream cones in a muffin
pan and help your little baker fill them two-thirds full
with cake batter in her favorite flavor. Bake according
to your recipe or the mix instructions. Let cool, then
help her frost the "cones" and add sprinkles.

320

teach an old dog a new trick

Your child will have a great time teaching the family dog some new moves by rewarding her behaviors as she gets closer and closer to what he wants her to do. For "shake," for instance, have him first reward the dog with a small treat and a "Good dog!" just for sitting down. Then he can take her paw and shake it, saying "Shake!" and giving praise and a treat. Eventually just saying "Shake!" should make the dog raise her paw. Give your pup lots of praise and the occasional treat, and she'll have the trick down pat.

321
sculpt ice

Help your child cool off on a hot day by using spoons and other blunt kitchen tools to chip and carve away at blocks of ice you've made by freezing water in clean milk cartons.

322
design finger puppets

Cut the fingers from an old knit glove and invite your child to use nontoxic markers and glue to decorate each of the fingers with ears, tails, faces, dragon scales, and other features made out of materials such as felt, yarn, sequins, and buttons. Then have a puppet show. Afterward, store the puppets in a bag—they're a perfect take-along diversion for a long car ride.

5+

5 years & up

323

look out for letters

Play "alphabet" lotto in the car. Challenge your child to find all the letters of the alphabet on the road signs that you pass during your trip.

324

make a banana octopus

Help your child make an eight-legged friend out of a banana. Have him wash an unpeeled banana, then help him cut eight slits in the bottom of the peel with kitchen shears. Show him how to pull the peel halfway back to lengthen the "tentacles," then help him cut off the exposed fruit with a butter knife for a snack. Have him stand the rest of the banana up and spread the tentacles around its base. Add raisins for eyes.

325

"so the pawn moves up a space... Chess is kind of hard, but I love playing a game that you love, too.**"**

5+

5 years & up

326

coil a pot

Show your child how to make a pot
by starting off with a disk of clay, then
making a long thin "snake" of clay to
coil around it, building higher with
every turn. She can leave the coil
visible or gently press and rub the
surface to make it smoother. If she
wants to make things permanent,
have her pot fired at a local kiln.

327

make chocolaty ghosts

Slowly melt a bag of white chocolate chips
in a double boiler (adult job). Pour the melted
chocolate into a large zip-top plastic bag and
snip a small opening in one bottom corner.
Once the bag cools enough to handle safely,
show your child how to squeeze gently to pipe
ghostly shapes onto parchment or wax paper.
While still soft, lay a lollipop stick (available
at cooking and crafts stores) into the chocolate,
and invite your child to add two semisweet
chocolate chips for eyes. When cool, wrap the
sweet spooks individually in plastic wrap and
store them in a cool place.

5+

5 years & up

328

get in some rhyme time

Five-year-olds are pretty adept with rhymes. Encourage that skill by giving your child rhyming books and asking him to try finishing some rhymes himself. Make things more challenging by asking targeted questions like "What rhymes with *big* and begins with a *p*?"

329

plant a terrarium

A widemouthed jar can become a great indoor garden. Show your child how to layer small pebbles with potting soil and plant fern and ivy cuttings or succulent seedlings. Have her finish the terrarium with a few decorative stones. Put her in charge of watering and making sure the plants are getting enough light.

330

celebrate butterflies

Invite your child to follow a butterfly (from a few feet away, so he doesn't frighten it) as it makes its rounds in your yard. Talk about what the butterfly is doing. Does it fly close to the ground or up high? What kinds of flowers does it like? Maybe you two can plant more of those plants in your yard to attract more butterflies. Back at home, your child can honor his new favorite insect with a "butterfly blot." Have him fold a piece of construction paper in half, cut out the curve of butterfly wings, and unfold the paper. Then he can apply nontoxic poster paint, refold the paper, then unfold it again. Once the paint dries, he'll have a colorful butterfly to hang on the wall or the refrigerator.

5+

5 years & up

331

name that animal

Hone your child's logical thinking and knowledge of nature with an animal guessing game. Give her a new clue after each incorrect guess. The game might go something like this:

"I'm thinking of an animal that lives in Africa."

"Is it a zebra?"

"No. It has spots, not stripes."

"A hyena?"

"No. It's a big cat."

"It's a leopard!"

"Right, it's a leopard!"

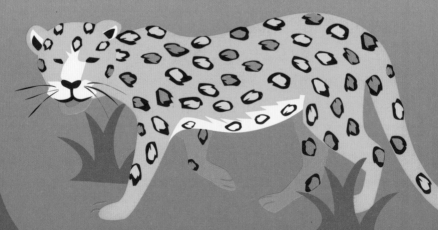

332

see what's in the sea

Take a small, two-handled drift net or mesh laundry bag to the beach, lake, or pond and see what you and your child can scoop up together. (Be sure to put any living creatures you catch back in the water quickly.)

333

5+

write a book

5 years & up

If your child sees other members of the family writing (letters, reports for work, homework), it will seem only natural for him to write, too. A blank journal is perfect for practicing writing the alphabet, doodling, and maybe even starting to write a few words and simple sentences. If he's looking for something to do, you can always suggest, "Why not work on your book?"

334

play a dance game

Turn on some peppy music and invite your little dancer to kick up his heels. Sway along, but stay close to the stereo so you can press pause at an unexpected moment and shout, "Freeze!" That's his clue to halt, holding his body still as if "frozen." Turn the music back on and let him continue his footloose antics.

335

hunt for treasure

Take photos of items around the house: a rocking chair on the porch, a potted plant on the windowsill, Teddy snoozing on your child's bed. Set up a treasure hunt, leaving photo "clues" for her to follow from one place to the next. Make sure to include a surprise at the end!

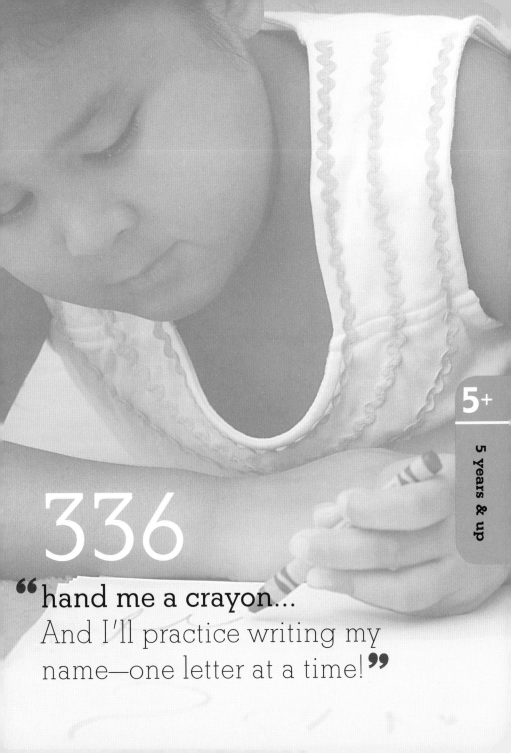

5+

5 years & up

336

" hand me a crayon...
And I'll practice writing my
name—one letter at a time! "

337

do more with dominos

Dominos are wonderful toys for five-year-olds. The game itself is simple to play: just follow the basic rules that come with a domino set. Dominos provide great practice in taking turns, counting groups of objects at a glance, recognizing patterns, and coming up with winning strategies. When the game's over, they're also great fun to build with.

338

help with chores

Kids this age get immense satisfaction from helping out, so put your child to work. Look for chores that are fairly easy, but stretch his logical and mathematical thinking. You might ask him to put the silverware away for you, sorting each piece into the right slot.

339

sing a buzz-off song

This song has a sweet message (unless you're a fly).

Shoo, fly, don't bother me,
Shoo, fly, don't bother me,
Shoo, fly, don't bother me,
For I belong to somebody.

340

assemble a cookie kit together

Have your child layer the makings for cookies in a widemouthed jar. Add each dry ingredient, such as chocolate chips, one at a time. Mix the flour with any salt, baking soda, or baking powder before adding. Ask your child to draw a picture of the cookie on a recipe card and attach (recipients add the wet ingredients).

341

design a family crest

Draw a large shield shape on stiff paper and invite your child to draw lines dividing the shield into three or four sections. Talk about items she could draw in those sections to represent things or activities that your family enjoys. Help her come up with a motto, something your family believes in or says often.

342

frame a picture

Have your child use nontoxic paints to make a picture on cardboard, leaving some space around the edges. Then have him use nontoxic glue to attach tiles (let him pick out his favorite colors at a crafts store), shells, or other treasures around the picture to frame it.

343

cut costs

Enlist your youngster's help in clipping coupons (lots of straight lines!) from weekend flyers. Explain how coupons help you save money, then go to the store and encourage your child to help find the bargain items.

344

color cats

Cut out cat shapes from colored construction paper and lay them in a shallow box. Have your child dip a large marble in colored paint and roll it over the paper cats, using different marbles for each color. When the paint dries, she can use nontoxic markers to add eyes, a nose, a mouth, and whiskers to each one.

345

ask probing questions

In "Twenty Questions," you provide clues to the identity of the person or object you're thinking of in answer to yes-or-no questions. The first question is traditionally "Animal, mineral, or vegetable?" A round might go something like this:

"Animal, mineral, or vegetable?"
"Animal."
"Is it a human being?"
"Yes."
"Is the person in the family?"
"Yes."
"Is the person tall?"
"Yes."
"Are you thinking of Uncle Ryan?"
"Yes!"

346

bake shortcakes

5+

5 years & up

Ask your child to help you measure, mix, roll, and cut biscuits (use your favorite recipe), adding a tablespoon of sugar along with the usual dry ingredients. Roll the dough out until it's ½ inch (1.25 cm) thick and cut out mini shortcakes with a large, round cookie cutter. Have him brush the tops with a little milk and sprinkle with a little more sugar. Bake according to the recipe. When the cakes are cool enough to eat, let your child split them open with a fork, cover with strawberries (or other fresh fruit), and top off with dollops of whipped cream.

347

fold a cup

Show your child how to make a usable cup from a square of paper. Working together, fold it in half to make a triangle. With the top of the triangle facing away from you, fold the left and right ends inward, so that they meet and overlap along a horizontal line underneath the top of the triangle. Fold the top flaps down in the front and back. Now he can open the cup!

348

make paper beads

Cut rectangles 3 inches (7.5 cm) long and of various widths from magazine pages, gift wrap, or origami paper. Have your child roll the paper around a pencil and glue closed with nontoxic glue. Slide off when dry. String a few of the beads to make a necklace.

349

climb a tree

For a five-year-old, a tree to climb is as good as a jungle gym. Look for a trunk with low, sturdy branches. Climbing clothes shouldn't have drawstrings, hoods, or anything that might get caught on a branch. Set a height limit, and stay nearby.

5+

5 years & up

350

get psyched for school

If your five-year-old's starting kindergarten this
year, it's a great idea to prepare her—especially
if she isn't used to leaving you to go to preschool
or day care. One way to build her enthusiasm for
the classroom is to set her up with materials like
a blackboard and books so she can play school.
Act the role of the teacher, then switch places so
she can teach you a thing or two. It's important to
get your child familiar with her new school. Take a
day trip together to the school she'll be attending,
highlighting aspects you know she'll think are
fun: the playground, the big yellow bus she'll
be riding, or the classroom where she'll have a
chance to do art projects and meet new playmates.

351

spot animal antics

Visit a zoo with your child and point out animals that illustrate the idea of camouflage. Do some critters use their markings—say, their stripes—to hide in their habitats? What do other animals use?

352

knit a toy snake

5+

5 years & up

Find an old-fashioned knitting spool (sometimes called a knitting knobby or knitting nancy) at a crafts shop and follow the directions, showing your child how to lift loops of yarn over the pins on top to knit a soft, woolly snake toy. Sew on some button eyes. He can also use the knitting spool to make knitted tubes for scarves or belts.

353

listen to simon

Teach your child to play "Simon Says" with
a group of friends. Have all the children face
the one who is "it," or Simon. That child then
dictates a simple activity for the others to do,
such as hopping on one foot or turning around
in a circle. The twist is that the activity should
be performed only if Simon begins by saying
"Simon says." Children who follow instructions
that don't start off with those words sit down and
wait for the next round. The last child standing
becomes the new Simon.

354

"tuck and roll... With your help and a safe spot, I can learn to somersault. **"**

355

catch an outdoor movie

During warm weather, check a community activities guide for outdoor movies. If you find one, take along a blanket and snacks and enjoy the show under the stars. Can't find an outdoor showing near where you live? Camp out on the family room floor with sleeping bags and popcorn while you watch a DVD or video.

356

watch the skies

Get your child into the sky-watching habit. Study
some posters or books about space together. Point
out the way the moon goes through different phases
every month. Help her find and track a constellation
that's easy to spot, such as Orion or the Big Dipper.

357

bake calzone

Teach your child to cook an Italian favorite using
a tube of refrigerated roll dough, a jar of pizza sauce,
and a little shredded mozzarella cheese. Have him
roll the dough into small circles, add a smear of sauce,
and finish with a sprinkle of cheese in the center.
Fold in half and crimp the edges, then bake the mini
calzone according to the dough directions.

358

make rock candy

Have your child put 2 cups (250 grams) of sugar and 1 cup (250 ml) of water into a pot. Bring to a boil (adults only), stirring constantly until the sugar dissolves. Cool slightly, pour into a clean glass jar, and cover with foil. Have your child carefully poke wooden skewers or chopsticks through the foil, not letting them touch the sides or bottom of the jar. After a week or so, sugar crystals will begin to grow on the sticks. Invite your child to track the crystals' growth. After another week, let her remove the homemade rock candy, study it, and eat it. Science can be tasty!

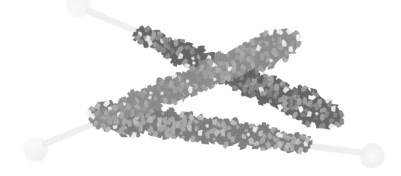

359

sing a song of grass

Kids get a kick out of this nonsensical folk song.

There was a hole in the middle of the ground,
The prettiest hole that you ever did see.

Well, the hole in the ground,
And the green grass grew all around and around,
And the green grass grew all around.

And in this hole there was a root,
The prettiest root that you ever did see.

Well, the root in the hole,
And the hole in the ground,
And the green grass grew all around and around,
And the green grass grew all around.

360
read a chapter book

Your child will still love his picture books for a long
time, but this is a good stage to introduce simple
chapter books. He can sit beside you or in your lap
and follow along as you read out loud. At bedtime,
snuggle with him in bed and read a short chapter
aloud, showing him the pictures and pointing out
simple, often-repeated words as you go along.

361
picture a shape

Have your child close her eyes, then touch a pencil tip
to a piece of paper. Challenge her to draw a circle or
other geometric shape in one motion, without peeking
or raising the pencil. It's only fair if you try it, too!

362

eat greek

Get your child to help you make a Greek salad. Have him tear iceberg lettuce into a bowl and add sliced tomatoes and cucumbers, pitted kalamata olives, and crumbled feta cheese. Help him measure dressing ingredients into a jar, seal it tight, and shake away.

363

play "grandma's attic"

Try out this memory game with a group of kids or the whole family. The first player begins: "In grandma's attic, there's an alligator." The next player adds an item beginning with the letter *b:* "In grandma's attic, there's an alligator and a baseball." Continue with the letters of the alphabet until one of the players can't recall all the previous items.

364

clap out haiku

Together with your child, read up on haiku: short, simple poems that often have nature themes. The structure for haiku—five syllables in the first line, seven in the second, and five in the third—makes for a fun game of syllable counting. Clap your hands with your child to mark each syllable, then try writing some of your own haiku together. Here's one example to get you clapping:

The busy bees buzz
in the back of the garden
where the daisies grow.

365

make a to-go art kit

Outfit your young artist with a traveling art kit. Fill a small backpack with a sketchbook, a watercolor pad, paintbrushes, colored pencils, a mini watercolor set, an artist's gum eraser, a small water bottle, and a plastic cup. He will have all the makings for a creative expedition to the woods, the shore—or just the backyard.

5+

5 years & up

index

a, b, c

d, e, f

g, h, i

j, k, l

m, n, o

about gymboree

Since 1976, Gymboree has helped parents and children discover the many pleasures and benefits of play. Based on established principles of early childhood education and administered by trained teachers, Gymboree Play & Music classes emphasize the wonder of play in a noncompetitive, nurturing environment. Gymboree, which runs its interactive parent-child programs in more than 29 countries, has contributed to the international awareness of the importance of play.

consulting editors

Dr. Roni Cohen Leiderman is a developmental psychologist specializing in emotional development, positive discipline, and play. For more than 25 years, she has worked with children, families, and professionals. She is associate dean of the Mailman Segal Institute for Early Childhood Studies at Nova Southeastern University in Fort Lauderdale, Florida, and the mother of two children.

Dr. Wendy Masi is a developmental psychologist specializing in early childhood. She has designed and implemented programs for preschools, families with young children, and early childhood professionals for more than 25 years. The mother of four children, Dr. Masi is dean of the Mailman Segal Institute for Early Childhood Studies at Nova Southeastern University.

author

Nancy Wilson Hall, the mother of two children, is the award-winning author of eight books about babies, children, and families.

illustrator

Christine Coirault, a children's book illustrator based in London, is the illustrator of How Do I Say That?, as well as the author of The Little Book of Good Manners.

photographer

John Robbins is a San Francisco–based photographer who has extensive experience working with kids. He has a five-year-old daughter and another on the way.